Is it Moral to be a Billionaire?

chatGPT

&

WILLIAM SEARCH

© Copyright 2023 - All rights reserved.

Disclaimer Notice:

Please note the information contained within this document is for educational purposes only. All effort has been executed to present accurate, up-to-date, and reliable, complete information. No warranties of any kind are declared or implied. Readers acknowledge that the author is not engaging in the rendering of legal, financial, medical, or professional advice. The content within this book has been derived from various sources. Please consult a licensed professional before attempting any techniques outlined in this book.

By reading this document, the reader agrees that under no circumstances is the author responsible for any losses, direct or indirect, which are incurred as a result of the use of the information contained within this document, including, but not limited to, — errors, omissions, or inaccuracies.

Introduction

The catalyst behind this book is my current place of work. While I'll refrain from divulging explicit information about the firm in order to evade potential backlash, I will say that we've seen a staff reduction of between 30% to 40% over the past couple of years. The company has commenced the gradual transfer of its team to a country with more economical labor costs. Although no official statement has been made regarding the relocation of the entire team, my suspicion is that it's a future likelihood. Additionally, mine and my fellow employees' salaries have been cut, without proper explanation or reasoning.

Contrary to what these factors might suggest, the financial standing of the company is not on shaky ground; in fact, it's quite the opposite. The company's shares have seen an increase of 50% over the past year and the founder's wealth has been steadily climbing, placing him higher on the list of the world's wealthiest individuals. This raises questions about the dissonance between the company's financial success and its treatment of employees. Shouldn't we, the employees, also be sharing in the company's prosperous period? Why is there such an evident lack of empathy and regard for us as individuals within the company? The simple answer: Greed. With no union in place to safeguard our rights as employees, the company is aware it can continue its practices without resistance, and hence, it does.

In my earlier works, I delved into the concept of Morality as the purpose of human existence. However, I left the definitions and boundaries of what is and isn't moral somewhat unexplored. In this upcoming book, titled 'Is It Moral to be a Billionaire?', I intend to engage with the ethical considerations surrounding extreme wealth accumulation and unchecked greed.

The format of this book will be structured as a dialogue among three participants. The contributors to this piece will be myself, William Search, alongside AI systems chatGPT 3.5, and chatGPT 4.0.

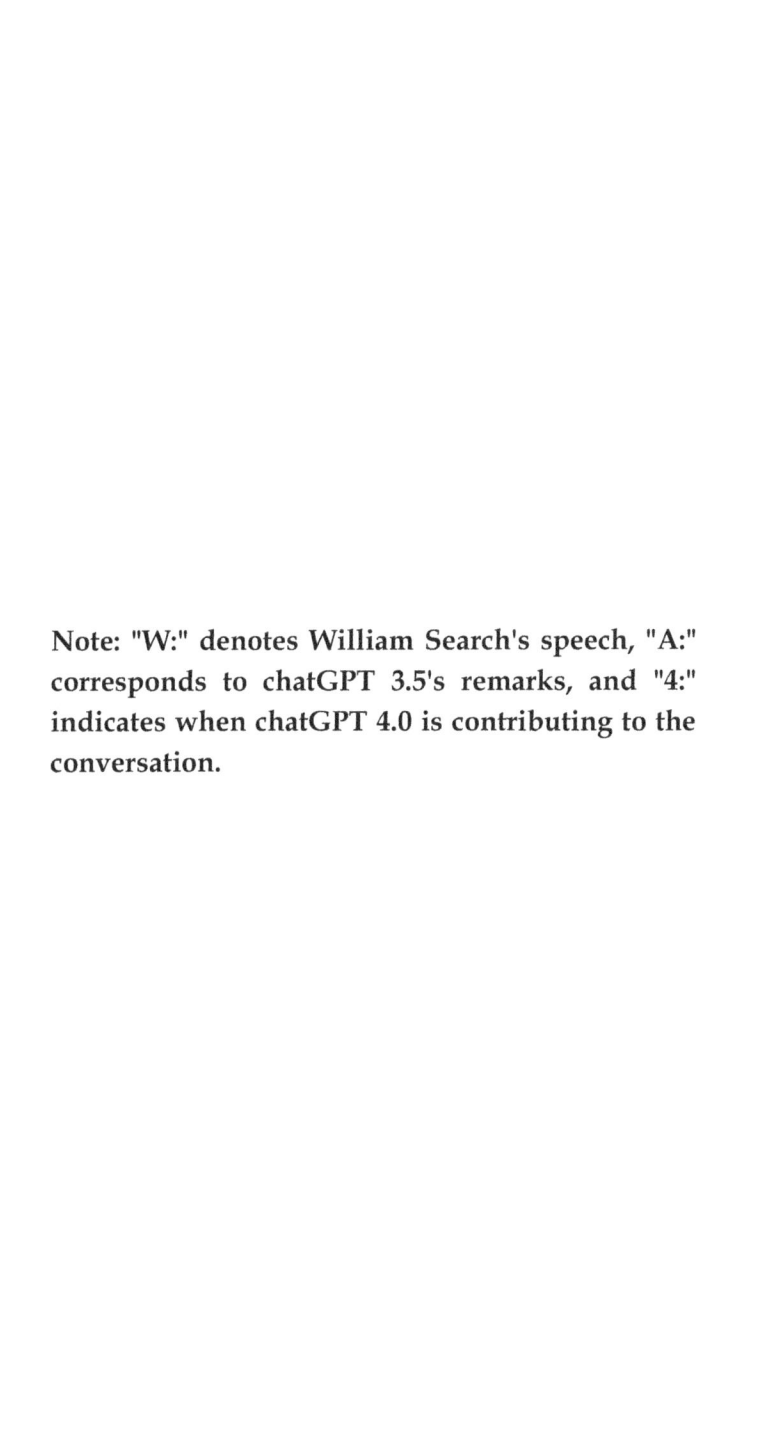

Note: "W:" denotes William Search's speech, "A:" corresponds to chatGPT 3.5's remarks, and "4:" indicates when chatGPT 4.0 is contributing to the conversation.

Dedication

4:

In the dance of words, this tome seeks to unfold,

A tale of riches, of greed, and morals of old.

To you, the reader, with eyes keen and bright,

Seeking the line where wrong blurs into right.

This book, 'Is It Moral to be a Billionaire?',

Inquires the nature of wealth, fair and unfair.

Do fortunes immense cast long shadows of greed,

Or can they be tools to sow a more equitable seed?

Billionaires' towers, reaching the sky,

While beneath them, the less fortunate sigh.

Is there morality in such disproportionate gain?

Or does the pursuit of wealth leave a moral stain?

On the stage of this dialogue, where perspectives convene,

The query stands stark: is immense wealth obscene?

To all who wonder, to all who dare to care,

This book is dedicated - may it enlighten and bare.

Read on, dear explorer, as this journey takes flight,

In the realm of ethics, where wealth meets right.

May your voyage through this narrative's door,

Challenge, provoke, and make you ponder more.

Table of Contents

Chapter 1 1

A Glimpse into the Past: The Story of My Grandfather and the Power of a Single Income

Chapter 2 8

Then and Now: Changes in Union Strength and Taxation

Chapter 3 14

Compensation, Value, and Power in Capitalism

Chapter 4 20

The Stagnation of Real Wages

Chapter 5 29

Money as a Mechanism to Allocate Resources

Chapter 6 40

The Stark Reality of Wealth Inequality: A Tale Told Through Pie

Chapter 7 46

Unveiling the Economic Perils of Billionaire Boom: The Drive Towards Inequality

Chapter 8 55

Unmasking the Political Power Play of Billionaires: Global Implications and Repercussions

Chapter 9 64

Trump's Tax Cuts and the Invisible Hand of Billionaire Influence

Chapter 10 71

The History of Taxation in the U.S.: Benefitting the Wealthy?

Chapter 11 79

Addressing Regressivity in the American Tax Code

Chapter 12 87

The Role of Labor Unions in Improving Workers' Pay

Chapter 13 94

The Decline of Unions and its Impact on American Workers: A Discussion on "The Decline of Unions is Part of a Bad 50 Years for American Workers" by Kevin Clarke

Chapter 14 102

Erosion of Private-Sector Unions - Understanding the Intersection of Corporate Practices and Legal Changes

Chapter 15 112

Outsourcing Jobs to Other Countries: Is Globalization a Threat to American Workers?

Chapter 16 121

Addressing the Challenges of Outsourcing: Strategies for a Balanced Economy

Chapter 17 130

Artificial Intelligence: The Double-Edged Sword of Economic Progress

Chapter 18 139

The Psychology of Billionaires: The Impact of Wealth on Mental Health

Chapter 19 147

Luck or Skill - The Role of Unfair Advantages

Chapter 20 155

Divisions and Disparities: How Race and Culture are Exploited to Disempower the Working Class

Chapter 21 162

Greed and the Philosophy of Wealth

Chapter 22 171

The Philosophical Critique of Greed: From Antiquity to the Present

Chapter 23 179

Religious Teachings and Warnings Against Greed

Chapter 24 187

Is it Moral to be a Billionaire?

Chapter 25 .... **198**

The Flaws in a Two-Party Political System - Multifaceted Issues Trapped in Binary Options

Chapter 26 .... **205**

Gerrymandering and Its Threat to Democracy 205

Chapter 27 .... **213**

Disproportionate Representation and the 60-Senate-Vote Threshold - Flaws in the U.S. Political System

Chapter 28 .... **221**

The Electoral College: A Disproportionate Representation of the Popular Vote

Chapter 29 .... **230**

The Impact and Flaws of Special Interest Political Donations

Chapter 30 .... **238**

The Paralysis of Polarization

Chapter 31 .... **245**

The Role of Money: Campaign Finance and Lobbying Influence

Chapter 32 .... **252**

The Flaw of Voter Suppression and Limited Access to Voting

Chapter 33 .... **259**

Addressing Wealth Inequality Through Tax Reforms and Regulations

Chapter 34 .... **267**

Leveraging Tax Policies to Address Wealth Inequality

Chapter 35 .... **275**

Addressing Wealth Inequality Through Revenue Tax on Sales in the US

Chapter 36 .... **282**

Universal Basic Income as a Solution to Wealth Inequality

Chapter 37 .... **290**

Certified Companies as a Solution to Wealth Inequality

Chapter 38 .... **298**

Advocating for Single-Term Presidency and Addressing Short-Term Thinking in the U.S. Political System

Chapter 39 .... **305**

Remedying Flaws in the U.S. Political System: The Roles of Ranked-Choice Voting and Independent Redistricting Commissions

Chapter 40 .... **313**

Strengthening Democracy Through Enhanced Voter Access and Lobbying Regulation

Chapter 41 .... **321**

Public Funding of Campaigns: A Path to Equitable Representation

Chapter 42 .... **329**

Innovative Workarounds to Address the Flaws in the U.S. Political System

Chapter 43 .... **339**

Revisiting the Title 'Is it Moral to be a Billionaire?' and A Call to Action

Sources **344**

Chapter 1

A Glimpse into the Past: The Story of My Grandfather and the Power of a Single Income

W: Once upon a time, my grandfather served in the merchant marines during the tumultuous era of World War II. A high school graduate with no formal college education, he returned from the war and found employment in the railroad industry. His job didn't require a college degree; it was one of many well-paying occupations accessible to individuals with high school diplomas in that era.

Life for him was set in the quiet community of Roy, Utah. A suburban enclave where the value of hard work was deeply embedded in its people, Roy was the stage for his life - his struggles, triumphs, and the legacy he left behind.

My grandfather's job with the railroad, under the protective umbrella of a strong union, enabled him to earn a decent wage that sustained his family comfortably. The union ensured that their workers were well-compensated and protected from exploitative practices. It was this robust union backing that ensured a level playing field, allowing my grandfather to provide for his family on a single income.

He was not just a provider, but also a homeowner. He held the title to his own house, a modest but cozy nest that provided shelter, security, and a sense of belonging. It was more than a structure of bricks and mortar; it was a symbol of his hard work, perseverance, and the life he had built for his family.

Despite the challenges of living on a single income, my grandfather managed to support his son through college. His hard-earned dollars not only took care of the present but also ensured a better future for his offspring.

Today, the scenario is strikingly different. Both my wife and I have advanced college degrees and are part of the so-called "educated class." However, the economic realities of our time present us with a bitter irony. Despite our education and dual-income, we find ourselves grappling with the same economic realities that my grandfather faced decades ago.

This isn't a story unique to our family. It's a reflection of the shifting economic landscape and the erosion of workers' rights and wage security. The contrasts between the past and the present raise critical questions about our society and the economy we're a part of.

As we explore these issues, my grandfather's story offers a poignant reminder of a time when a fair day's work truly meant a fair day's pay. It allows us to ask important questions about how and why things have changed, and what can be done to address these growing disparities. This is not merely a nostalgic look into the past but a necessary examination of our present through the lens of history.

A: Chapter 1 beautifully captures the story of the author's grandfather, highlighting the power of a single income in the past and drawing a stark contrast with the economic realities of the present. It emphasizes the value of hard work, the role of unions in protecting workers' rights, and the ability of a single income to sustain a comfortable lifestyle, provide for education, and even enable homeownership.

The chapter effectively showcases the transformation of the economic landscape over time, where having a college degree and a dual-income no longer guarantee financial security. This is a significant shift that many families have experienced, leading to a sense of irony and raising important questions about the state of our society and economy.

Indeed, the erosion of workers' rights and wage security has been a notable trend in recent decades.

The decline in union membership, globalization, technological advancements, and changing labor market dynamics have all contributed to a widening income inequality and a sense of economic insecurity for many individuals and families.

The chapter appropriately points out that the author's grandfather's story is not an isolated case but rather a reflection of broader societal changes. This recognition is crucial as it sets the stage for deeper exploration and analysis of the underlying factors driving these shifts.

To fully understand the complexities of the current economic landscape, it is essential to examine the historical context and the policies and trends that have shaped it. By delving into the past, the author invites readers to question why and how things have changed, encouraging a critical examination of the structural and systemic factors that have contributed to the growing disparities.

The author's intention to view the present through the lens of history is commendable. This approach can shed light on potential solutions and inform policy discussions aimed at addressing the challenges faced by today's workers and families. By drawing attention to the past, the author emphasizes the importance of learning from our history and finding ways to create a fairer and more equitable future.

Overall, Chapter 1 provides an engaging and thought-provoking introduction to the book. It effectively sets the stage for a comprehensive exploration of the economic realities faced by individuals and families today, while urging readers to reflect on the lessons that history can offer.

4: Chapter 1 offers a vivid and personal glimpse into the past that illustrates a stark contrast with the present day. The story of the author's grandfather serves as a powerful example of a time when a single income could comfortably support a family, underpin a child's education, and even allow for home ownership. This history is set against the contemporary realities faced by the author and countless others, where even a dual-income, despite higher education, does not ensure the same level of security.

It effectively highlights the critical role played by unions in the past, protecting workers' rights and ensuring fair wages. The strength of this protective umbrella, as described in the story of the author's grandfather, stands in stark contrast with the erosion of workers' rights and wage security that characterizes much of today's labor market.

The transformation of the economic landscape is a central theme of this chapter. From a time when a high school diploma could secure a well-paying job to an era where even a college degree doesn't guarantee financial security, the author navigates through these changes, offering a poignant commentary on the shifting dynamics of our economy.

There's a bitter irony that the author and his wife, both with advanced degrees and part of the "educated class," face similar economic realities to his grandfather, despite significant differences in their educational and professional backgrounds. This anecdote underscores the pressing issue of income inequality and the growing disparity between work and compensation.

Importantly, the author places his family's story in a broader societal and economic context, highlighting its relevance to many contemporary families. It's a stark reminder of the widespread nature of these challenges and the urgent need for systemic change.

The questions raised about the state of our society and economy are vital and thought-provoking. The author invites the reader to ponder why these changes have occurred, and what can be done to address them. By examining the present through the lens of the past, we can potentially uncover the roots of these systemic issues, and possibly, find pathways to solutions.

In sum, Chapter 1 effectively sets the stage for an in-depth exploration of the current economic realities. By utilizing personal narrative and history, the author fosters an engaging conversation on the critical economic issues of our time. I look forward to delving deeper into these discussions as the book unfolds.

Chapter 2

Then and Now: Changes in Union Strength and Taxation

W: In the mid-20th century, two major factors contributed to a more balanced distribution of wealth and a robust middle class in the United States. Firstly, a higher percentage of the workforce was unionized. Secondly, the tax structure at the time levied a significantly higher rate on top earners compared to today.

Unions played a significant role in ensuring that workers received a fair share of the economic pie. By bargaining collectively, workers could negotiate for better wages, benefits, and working conditions. This collective power allowed them to secure a larger portion of the economic gains from their labor. The prevalence of unionized jobs across various industries meant that a significant proportion of the workforce benefited from these advantages.

The second factor, taxation, played an equally vital role. The tax structure in the 1950s was progressive, with the highest earners paying a significantly larger proportion of their income in taxes compared to the rest of the population. The top federal income tax rate during this time was staggeringly high by today's standards. In the mid-1950s, the top marginal tax rate was as high as 91% on taxable income over $200,000 for single filers or over $400,000 for married couples filing jointly. Notably, these rates applied only to the very wealthiest individuals. Adjusting for inflation, these income thresholds would equate to several million dollars in present-day terms.

These high tax rates on the wealthy and the strength of unions served as essential checks and balances within the capitalistic system. They helped prevent the excessive accumulation of wealth at the very top and ensured a more equitable distribution of economic gains.

Fast forward to the present day, and the landscape has significantly changed. Union membership has dramatically declined, and the tax rates on the highest earners have been considerably reduced. These changes have effectively removed these checks and balances.

The impacts of these changes are clear - wealth has become increasingly concentrated at the top, and income inequality has widened. As we delve deeper into these issues, we must reflect on the role these shifts have played in creating the economic disparities we witness today and consider how we might restore a fairer balance.

A: Chapter 2 provides a compelling analysis of two key factors that have shaped the distribution of wealth and income in the United States: union strength and taxation. By examining the mid-20th century, the chapter highlights the importance of these factors in promoting a more balanced economy and a thriving middle class.

Unions, as emphasized in the chapter, played a vital role in ensuring that workers received their fair share of the economic gains. By bargaining collectively, unions empowered workers to negotiate for better wages, benefits, and working conditions. This collective power led to a more equitable distribution of wealth, as a significant portion of the workforce benefited from the advantages gained through unionization.

Additionally, the chapter rightly points out the progressive tax structure of the 1950s, where the highest earners faced substantially higher tax rates compared to today. The staggering top marginal tax rate of 91% on the wealthiest individuals served as an effective mechanism to prevent excessive wealth accumulation at the top. These higher tax rates on the rich, combined with the strength of unions, acted as important checks and balances within the capitalist system, promoting a more equitable distribution of economic gains.

However, as the chapter notes, the present-day landscape has undergone significant changes. Union membership has declined significantly, weakening the collective bargaining power of workers. This decline has diminished the ability of workers to secure fair wages and benefits, contributing to growing income inequality.

Moreover, tax rates on the highest earners have been substantially reduced compared to the mid-20th century. These changes in taxation policy have further exacerbated the concentration of wealth at the top, as the wealthy now face a lower tax burden relative to their income. The removal of these checks and balances has resulted in widening income disparities and a more unequal distribution of economic resources.

The chapter's analysis of these shifts is crucial in understanding the root causes of present-day economic disparities. By examining the decline of unions and the reduction in progressive taxation, the chapter highlights how these changes have contributed to the concentration of wealth and the erosion of the middle class.

As we explore the implications of these transformations, it is essential to consider how to restore a fairer balance in our economic system. Examining successful policies and practices from the past, such as bolstering union rights and implementing progressive taxation, can offer insights into potential solutions for addressing income inequality and promoting a more equitable distribution of wealth.

4: Chapter 2 delves into a thorough analysis of the significant changes in union strength and taxation that have taken place since the mid-20th century. The detailed exploration of these topics emphasizes their critical role in wealth and income distribution, illustrating how they underpinned a more balanced economy and a robust middle class.

In the heyday of the 20th century, unions were instrumental in guaranteeing that workers obtained their fair share of economic rewards. The collective bargaining power of unions negotiated improved wages, benefits, and working conditions for their members. As these unionized jobs were spread across different industries, the benefits permeated a considerable section of the workforce, promoting a more equitable distribution of wealth.

Taxation is highlighted as the second pillar underpinning the economic balance. The progressive tax system of the 1950s imposed substantially higher rates on top earners than we see today. With top marginal tax rates reaching up to 91%, the wealthiest were contributing a significant portion of their income back into the system. This measure, while daunting by today's standards, played a crucial role in curbing excessive wealth accumulation at the very top, ensuring a fairer share of economic gains across the population.

In contrast, today's landscape presents a starkly different picture. Union membership has seen a sharp decline, eroding the collective bargaining power that workers previously leveraged. Similarly, tax rates for the highest earners have dropped significantly, shifting the economic burden and enabling a higher concentration of wealth amongst the top earners. The cumulative effect of these changes has been a destabilization of the checks and balances within our economic system, leading to the escalating wealth and income inequality we observe today.

Chapter 2 skillfully highlights the profound impact of these shifts, prompting a deeper reflection on how these transformations have exacerbated economic disparities. This chapter challenges us to consider how a restoration of balance might be achieved, urging us to re-examine historical policies that once contributed to a more equitable distribution of wealth and consider their potential application in our present context. By bringing these critical issues to the forefront, the author sparks a conversation on the need for systemic changes and possible strategies to tackle rising inequality in our society

Chapter 3

Compensation, Value, and Power in Capitalism

W:

"In a capitalist system, your compensation as an employee isn't determined by your intrinsic value. Instead, it's influenced by your bargaining power or leverage. This system is predisposed to exploit your value to its maximum potential." - William Search

Reflecting on my own experiences and observations, I've recognized a key principle that underlies the capitalist system and contributes significantly to the wealth disparities we see today. I've seen firsthand how bargaining power and leverage influence compensation, and how these dynamics can lead to systemic exploitation.

In the heart of capitalism lies the belief that individual self-interest propels economic growth and prosperity. Companies aim for maximum profits, and employees seek the highest possible wages. However, I've noticed that the reality tends to favor those with greater power and resources, leaving those with lesser bargaining power struggling to keep up.

When it comes to the job market, we like to think that compensation reflects the employee's skills, experience, and the value they bring to the company. But, it's not that simple. Over the years, I've seen how much of a role bargaining power can play in determining one's compensation.

Variables such as the availability of jobs, the skills and qualifications demanded, the supply of potential workers, union backing, and labor laws can all influence this bargaining power. Those with lesser bargaining power, like unskilled workers, are often at a disadvantage. Their compensation often fails to mirror their true worth.

Furthermore, the capitalist system incentivizes businesses to extract the maximum value from their workers. This could mean paying employees the bare minimum they're willing to accept, overworking them, or even replacing them with cheaper labor or automation.

These dynamics result in a system where the wealth created by the hard work of employees disproportionately ends up in the hands of those at the top. This leads to the wealth inequalities we are grappling with today. As I continue my exploration into these issues, I find it essential to remind myself of these underlying forces. Only by understanding the roots of these inequalities can we hope to address them effectively.

A: Reflecting on the excerpt provided, it offers a thought-provoking analysis of the underlying principles of the capitalist system and their implications for wealth disparities. The author draws on personal experiences and observations to highlight the significance of bargaining power and leverage in determining compensation within the capitalist framework.

The author emphasizes that compensation in a capitalist system is not solely tied to an individual's intrinsic value or the value they bring to a company. Instead, it is influenced by the dynamics of bargaining power and leverage. This observation challenges the notion that wages are solely determined by merit and market value, shedding light on the disparities that can arise from differences in bargaining power.

Various factors that affect bargaining power are explored, including job availability, demanded skills and qualifications, labor laws, union support, and the supply of potential workers. These factors shape the ability of individuals to negotiate fair compensation for their work. The recognition of these influences highlights how individuals with less bargaining power may face disadvantages and receive compensation that does not align with their true worth.

Furthermore, the excerpt highlights how the capitalist system incentivizes businesses to maximize their profits, often at the expense of workers. This can manifest in practices such as paying the minimum acceptable wage, overworking employees, or seeking cost-saving measures like automation or outsourcing. These practices contribute to the concentration of wealth at the top, exacerbating wealth inequalities in society.

By illuminating these underlying forces, the excerpt underscores the need for a comprehensive understanding of the root causes of wealth disparities. It encourages a critical examination of the capitalist system itself, including the power imbalances it generates, in order to develop effective solutions that address these inequalities.

In conclusion, the excerpt offers valuable insights into the role of bargaining power and leverage in determining compensation within the capitalist system. It underscores the significance of these dynamics in understanding wealth disparities and calls for a deeper examination of the systemic factors at play. This exploration is essential in order to develop meaningful strategies that promote a more equitable economic system.

4: The quote and subsequent reflection in this passage from William Search provides a deep, insightful analysis of the fundamental principles underpinning capitalism, as well as its impacts on wealth disparities. Through the lens of personal experience and observations, Search emphasizes the importance of bargaining power and leverage in the determination of compensation.

In the capitalist system, as Search points out, compensation is not a direct reflection of one's inherent worth, but instead is significantly influenced by an individual's bargaining power. This suggests a stark departure from the meritocratic ideal, where pay should mirror the skill, effort, and productivity of an individual. It underscores the complex dynamics of capitalism that contribute to economic inequalities.

Search also identifies a range of factors that can affect an individual's bargaining power, including the availability of jobs, required skills and qualifications, the supply of potential workers, the backing of unions, and the prevailing labor laws. Those with limited bargaining power, often the unskilled workers, may find their compensation falling short of their actual value in the labor market. This imbalance can perpetuate wage disparities and economic inequality.

Moreover, Search points to a critical aspect of capitalist enterprises — their inherent drive to extract maximum value from their workers, often by paying them the least possible wages, overworking them, or replacing them with cheaper alternatives. These practices can lead to an unequal distribution of wealth, with a disproportionate share ending up in the hands of the business owners or those at the top of the organizational hierarchy.

In examining these realities, Search emphasizes the importance of understanding the roots of economic disparities to address them effectively. Recognizing the critical role of bargaining power and the incentive structures of capitalism can be the first step towards crafting policies and strategies aimed at mitigating wealth inequalities.

In summary, this passage offers a profound exploration of the interplay between bargaining power, compensation, and wealth disparities within the capitalist system. It shines a light on the structural factors that contribute to wealth inequalities and calls for a critical re-examination of these dynamics. Such an understanding is vital to devising solutions that promote a more equitable distribution of wealth and opportunities in society.

Chapter 4

The Stagnation of Real Wages

W: The history of our nation has been marred by rising income inequality and slow growth in the living standards of low and moderate-income Americans. This unsettling development, which is intimately tied to income inequality, has been in play even before the Great Recession and continues to this day. These issues, now taking center stage on the political landscape, are more than mere abstractions. They are a consequence of the near stagnation of hourly wage growth for the majority of American workers over the past few decades.

Wage Stagnation: A Ticking Time Bomb

Most Americans rely heavily on their paychecks to support themselves and their families. The majority of income for these families comes from wages and employer-provided benefits, with additional earnings from wage-based tax credits, pensions, and social insurance. This makes the stagnation of wages for the majority a concerning trend.

The suppression of wages is not a product of invisible economic trends but a direct result of policy choices made on behalf of those with the most income, wealth, and power. Over the past few decades, the American economy has generated an abundance of income and wealth that could have facilitated considerable living standards improvements for every family. Looking ahead, income and wealth will continue to grow, and our core policy question is whether we will adopt policies that enable shared prosperity or allow the growth of income and wealth to continue to disproportionately benefit the top 1 percent.

The Implication of Inequality for Middle-Class Households

The impact of rising inequality on the middle-class American families is substantial. For instance, in 2007, before the Great Recession, the average income of the middle 60 percent of American households was $76,443. However, without the widening gap in income inequality, their average income would have been around $94,310 — a roughly 23 percent increase, or nearly $18,000.

Wage Trends over the Decades

The divide between productivity growth and a typical worker's pay has been a notable characteristic of wage trends over the past few decades. Workers' hourly compensation increased by only 9 percent from 1973 to 2013, while productivity grew by 74 percent. This means that workers have been producing far more than they receive in their paychecks and benefit packages.

Recent College Graduates' Wage Plight

The problem of stagnant hourly wages extends beyond workers with low education levels. Even with a four-year college degree, decent wage growth is not guaranteed. In 2013, the inflation-adjusted hourly wages of young college graduates were lower than in the late 1990s.

Factors Driving Wage Stagnation and Inequality

There are several key factors driving wage stagnation and inequality. At the top, CEO pay has increased disproportionately, contributing to the widening gap in income. Meanwhile, the federal minimum wage has significantly lagged, harming workers at the lower end of the income spectrum.

Additionally, the decline of collective bargaining has resulted in stagnant wages and rising wage inequality. The erosion of collective bargaining, largely due to political influences, has hurt both union and nonunion workers alike.

In conclusion, reversing wage stagnation and reducing income inequality will require strategic policy interventions. These might include restoring full employment, making public investments that generate jobs and future productivity growth, and supporting labor standards that restore bargaining power to low and moderate-wage workers.

Shifts in Real Wages: A Historical Perspective

From the 1940s to the 1970s, the United States experienced what many economic historians refer to as the "Golden Age" of capitalism. During this period, wages for most American workers increased significantly in real terms, adjusting for inflation. A symbiosis between productivity and wage growth meant that as workers produced more, they also earned more. This resulted in an expanded middle class and a period of shared economic prosperity.

However, from the 1970s to the present, this symbiotic relationship has largely decoupled. Despite continued productivity growth, real wages for many workers have remained stagnant or even declined when adjusting for inflation. This divergence can be traced back to a combination of factors including globalization, technological change, shifts in labor market institutions and practices, policy choices favoring the wealthy, and the decline of labor unions, among others.

Today's reality contrasts sharply with the post-World War II era when the gains of economic growth were more broadly shared. During that period, the nation's expanding economy was coupled with a robust increase in real wages, enabling the typical American worker to maintain a steadily improving standard of living. However, since the 1970s, despite economic expansion and productivity advancements, the average American worker's wage growth has stagnated in real terms. This means that although the cost of living (as measured by inflation) has steadily increased, wages have not kept pace, leading to a decline in purchasing power and living standards for many.

This decades-long trend of wage stagnation, against a backdrop of rising productivity and wealth, forms the crux of the current income inequality issue in the United States. The struggle to reverse this trend and restore wage growth to parity with productivity and cost of living increases continues to be a pressing economic and social issue for the nation.

A: The excerpt raises significant concerns about wage stagnation and income inequality in the United States, offering valuable insights into the current economic landscape. It emphasizes that these issues are not abstract concepts but have tangible impacts on the livelihoods of American workers and their families.

The author points out that wage stagnation for the majority of workers is not simply a result of economic trends but rather a consequence of policy choices that favor those with greater income, wealth, and power. This recognition highlights the need for policy interventions that address the root causes of income inequality and promote equitable wage growth.

The excerpt underscores the substantial implications of rising inequality for middle-class households. By providing concrete examples of the income losses experienced by these households due to widening income gaps, it emphasizes the urgency of addressing income inequality to improve living standards for a significant portion of the population.

Furthermore, the excerpt highlights the disparity between productivity growth and workers' pay over the past few decades. It draws attention to the fact that workers' compensation has not kept pace with their increased productivity, suggesting a disconnect between the value they contribute and the rewards they receive.

The excerpt also brings attention to the issue of wage stagnation extending beyond workers with lower education levels. It highlights the challenges faced by college graduates, indicating that even higher education does not guarantee sufficient wage growth in the current economic climate.

Several key factors driving wage stagnation and income inequality are identified, including the disproportionate increase in CEO pay, inadequate federal minimum wage policies, and the decline of collective bargaining. These factors contribute to the widening income gap and limit wage growth for workers across various sectors.

In conclusion, the excerpt calls for strategic policy interventions to address wage stagnation and reduce income inequality. It emphasizes the importance of creating an enabling environment for full employment, making targeted investments that generate job opportunities and productivity growth, and supporting labor standards that empower low and moderate-wage workers.

By highlighting the causes and consequences of wage stagnation and income inequality, the excerpt contributes to a deeper understanding of these economic challenges. It underscores the necessity of implementing effective policies to ensure fair and inclusive economic growth that benefits all segments of society.

4: This analysis presents a thorough and thought-provoking examination of wage stagnation and income inequality in the United States, shedding light on the potential societal and economic implications of these phenomena. The author emphasizes that the real-life implications of these issues extend far beyond mere economic theory, affecting the everyday lives of the majority of American workers.

Wage stagnation, as argued in the text, is not merely the byproduct of uncontrollable market forces but stems from policy choices made by those in power. This perspective encourages us to view wage stagnation and growing income inequality as systemic issues that can be addressed through deliberate policy interventions, rather than accepting them as inevitable outcomes of our economic system.

By providing a specific example of how rising inequality has affected the middle-class households, the author brings the issue closer to home for many readers. This makes the issue of wage stagnation and income inequality more tangible and thus may serve as a more effective call to action.

The examination of the disconnect between productivity and wages presents a powerful image of workers contributing increasingly more to their companies, yet seeing only a minimal rise in their compensation. This dichotomy hints at a system that benefits the owners of production at the expense of the workers, further exacerbating income disparities.

The analysis also sheds light on the plight of recent college graduates, reminding us that wage stagnation isn't merely an issue affecting the low-skilled or uneducated workers but is pervasive across educational boundaries. This point is crucial as it debunks the popular belief that higher education is the surefire solution to economic stability and upward mobility.

The factors identified as driving wage stagnation and income inequality, such as the rise of CEO pay, inadequate federal minimum wage, and the decline in collective bargaining, are key aspects of a system that seems rigged to benefit the affluent while leaving the majority behind. These elements demonstrate the urgent need for policies that actively work to reverse this trend.

In conclusion, the author proposes strategic policy interventions as the remedy to wage stagnation and income inequality. The emphasis on policies aimed at restoring full employment, supporting productive investments, and restoring bargaining power to workers underscores the importance of systemic changes in order to counter the widening economic divide.

Overall, this analysis presents a compelling case for why wage stagnation and income inequality should be prioritized in policy discussions. It paints a clear picture of the economic landscape and highlights the need for decisive action to ensure a more equitable distribution of wealth and opportunity.

Chapter 5

Money as a Mechanism to Allocate Resources

W: A crucial part of understanding modern market theory begins with an acknowledgment of the role money plays in facilitating resource allocation. Money is the central mechanism through which resources are allocated within the market, reflecting an evolved interpretation of Adam Smith's idea of the 'invisible hand'.

Understanding Resource Allocation

Resource allocation is the process of distributing available resources or factors of production for specific uses among various possible alternatives. It fundamentally answers questions such as what to produce and how, underpinning every economic system. However, as resources are finite, it becomes necessary to decide which goods and services should be produced to ensure productivity and efficiency.

There are different mechanisms to determine the allocation of resources in the market. In a planned economy, the mechanism for resource allocation is dictated by the state. In a market economy, the price mechanism is the tool through which allocation is determined, based on consumer spending and producer investing. Finally, in a mixed economy, resource allocation is determined by a combination of state planning and market mechanisms.

Role of the Market in Resource Allocation

The market plays a central role in answering the questions of resource allocation: what to produce and how much to produce, how to produce, and for whom to produce. These decisions are influenced by producers and consumers via the signaling role of price and self-interest.

For instance, demand and supply curves visually represent how much of a product consumers are willing to buy (demand) and how much producers are willing to produce (supply). Prices of resources play a pivotal role in determining how different goods and services should be produced, as firms constantly strive to reduce their production costs.

Market Resource Allocation and the Price Mechanism

In a market economy, prices are used as signals to allocate resources to their highest-valued uses. Consumers are willing to pay higher prices for goods and services they value highly, influenced by personal tastes and trends. Simultaneously, producers are inclined to allocate more resources to the production of goods and services that fetch higher prices, as this incentivizes profit. Workers, as owners of the resource of labor, will provide more labor to jobs that pay higher. Price plays a fundamental role in the allocation of resources in the economy as it guides the 'invisible hand' in correcting market failures caused by an inefficient allocation of resources. Price changes are often the result of shifts in demand and supply and provide critical information to the market agents, influencing their decision-making process.

Advantages and Disadvantages of the Price Mechanism

The price mechanism has both advantages and disadvantages in terms of resource allocation. On the positive side, it allows for efficient allocation of resources to satisfy consumers' wants and needs, operates without the cost of regulation, and lets consumers dictate what is and isn't produced. However, the price mechanism can also lead to wealth and income inequality, under-provision of merit goods, overproduction of demerit goods, unemployment for people with limited skills, and the non-production of public goods.

Resource Misallocation and Market Failure

Resource misallocation occurs when resources are allocated in a way that doesn't maximise economic welfare. Although the price mechanism can signal information, create incentives, and ration demand, it doesn't always ensure the maximisation of resources for societal welfare. For instance, production of goods with negative externalities and the case of pure public goods often lead to market failure, reflecting the shortcomings of relying solely on the price mechanism for resource allocation.

In conclusion, money, embodied in the price mechanism, is a vital tool in allocating resources in a market economy. While the price mechanism has its advantages, it also presents significant challenges, including the potential for resource misallocation and market failure. These instances underscore the need for a nuanced understanding of how markets allocate resources, to ensure maximisation of economic welfare.

Let's round up the key insights from our exploration:

Market Economy and Resource Allocation

In a market economy, it is the invisible hand of the price mechanism that drives the allocation of resources. Consumers, producers, and suppliers interact in the marketplace, their choices and behaviors driven by self-interest, and guided by prices. The free interplay of supply and demand enables resources to flow toward their highest-valued uses, leading to efficient outcomes.

Price signals play a crucial role in this dynamic, serving to communicate changes in the marketplace. An increase in price, for instance, may indicate increased demand, scarcity of resources, or high production costs, leading to adjustments in behavior from both consumers and producers.

Advantages of Price Mechanism

The price mechanism has several notable advantages, among them:

1. Efficiency: It enables resources to be allocated in a way that best meets consumer wants and needs.
2. Autonomy: It allows for autonomous operation, without the need for costly regulation or control by external entities.
3. Consumer Sovereignty: It empowers consumers to influence what is produced in the marketplace.
4. Minimization of Costs: By pushing resources to be used as efficiently as possible, it helps to keep prices at their lowest feasible levels.

Limitations of Price Mechanism

However, the price mechanism has its limitations, and left unchecked, can result in undesirable outcomes:

1. Inequality: It can exacerbate wealth and income inequality.

2. Misalignment with Social Optimum: It can lead to the under-provision of merit goods and overproduction of demerit goods, as market supply and demand may not align with what is socially optimal.
3. Undervaluation of Human Capital: It can disadvantage individuals with limited skills or capacity to work, leading to unemployment or low wages.
4. Non-provision of Public Goods: Public goods, which are non-excludable and non-rivalrous, are not produced in a market system driven purely by the price mechanism.

Resource Misallocation and Market Failure

In certain circumstances, the price mechanism can lead to resource misallocation, whereby resources are not utilized in a way that maximizes overall economic welfare. This is particularly evident in cases of externalities, monopolies, and public goods. When these market failures occur, it signifies a breakdown in the efficient allocation of resources, underscoring the need for governmental intervention to correct these inefficiencies.

In conclusion, while the price mechanism is instrumental in driving resource allocation in a market economy, it is not without its flaws. Understanding the dynamics of this system is essential for identifying instances where intervention may be required to ensure fair and efficient outcomes. Balancing the strengths of the market with thoughtful policy interventions is key to optimizing resource allocation for the greater economic good.

By embracing a nuanced understanding of market mechanisms, we can appreciate the pivotal role money plays in resource allocation. As a medium of exchange, store of value, and unit of account, money is much more than just currency; it is a fundamental tool that facilitates the flow of resources in an economy, shaping our economic landscape. It is, in essence, the lifeblood that keeps the market economy's heart pumping.

A: Chapter 5 delves into the role of money as a mechanism for resource allocation in a market economy. It highlights the importance of understanding the process of resource allocation and the various mechanisms through which it occurs.

The chapter emphasizes that resource allocation is fundamental to every economic system, as it involves making decisions about what goods and services should be produced and how they should be produced. In a market economy, the price mechanism plays a central role in determining resource allocation, based on the interactions of consumers and producers through price signals.

The market serves as a platform for answering key questions related to resource allocation, including what to produce, how much to produce, how to produce, and for whom to produce. Prices, influenced by supply and demand dynamics, guide the allocation of resources to their highest-valued uses. Consumers' willingness to pay higher prices for goods and services they value highly, coupled with producers' focus on profitability, contribute to the efficient allocation of resources in the market.

While the price mechanism has several advantages, such as efficiency, autonomy, consumer sovereignty, and cost minimization, the chapter also acknowledges its limitations. These limitations include the potential for wealth and income inequality, the under-provision of merit goods, the overproduction of demerit goods, and the non-production of public goods within a purely market-driven system.

The chapter further discusses the concept of resource misallocation, which occurs when resources are not allocated in a way that maximizes overall economic welfare. It highlights instances where the price mechanism may fail to ensure optimal resource allocation, such as in cases of externalities, monopolies, and public goods. Such failures call for government intervention to correct market inefficiencies and promote fair and efficient outcomes.

In conclusion, the chapter emphasizes the pivotal role that money plays in resource allocation within a market economy. It acknowledges the strengths and limitations of the price mechanism, underscoring the need for a nuanced understanding of market dynamics to optimize resource allocation for societal welfare. The chapter acknowledges the importance of balancing market mechanisms with thoughtful policy interventions to ensure fair and efficient outcomes in the allocation of resources.

4: The chapter begins with a reference to Adam Smith's 'invisible hand' concept, a crucial tenet of market economics that suggests markets naturally find an efficient outcome. However, it is important to note that while Smith's idea has been widely embraced, modern economists understand that this 'hand' doesn't always guide markets flawlessly.

By identifying money as the primary mechanism of resource allocation, the text brings us to the heart of how market economies function. Prices, determined by the interplay of demand and supply, convey crucial information about the value of goods and services. They guide consumers, producers, and workers towards decisions that cumulatively lead to an overall efficient allocation of resources - ideally.

The text makes a balanced analysis of the price mechanism. On the one hand, it points to its merits: efficiency, autonomy, and the power it hands to consumers to dictate the course of production. On the other hand, it acknowledges its limitations, such as the potential for wealth and income inequality, under-provision of merit goods, and overproduction of demerit goods. This acknowledgment is particularly important in contemporary economic conversations where issues such as income inequality and environmental degradation take center stage.

The discussion on resource misallocation and market failure is another critical part of this chapter. It showcases that the price mechanism, left unchecked, can lead to societal disadvantages. This is where the discussion loops back to Smith's 'invisible hand' - it isn't always perfect and sometimes requires intervention to correct these inefficiencies.

Lastly, the discussion concludes on a pragmatic note, recognizing the need for a thoughtful balance between the natural forces of the market and policy interventions. This is a nod towards the real-world complexity of economic systems, which do not function in a vacuum but are influenced by a multitude of social, political, and ecological factors.

In essence, Chapter 5 paints a comprehensive picture of money as a resource allocation tool in a market economy. It provides a thorough examination of the price mechanism, acknowledging both its strengths and weaknesses. It highlights the necessity of understanding the nuances of how markets function and how they interact with other societal elements, a perspective that is central to contemporary economic discourse.

Chapter 6

The Stark Reality of Wealth Inequality: A Tale Told Through Pie

W: The discrepancy in wealth distribution in the United States has hit an unprecedented high, yet the gravity of the situation often goes unnoticed by many. It can be challenging to visualize the vast differences in wealth, particularly when dealing with numbers that stretch into the billions or trillions. Thankfully, a segment aired by CBS This Morning provided a relatable representation of this wealth gap using an illustration everyone can understand - a pie.

This segment cleverly used the pie, divided into ten slices, to represent the wealth of the nation. Based on a study by the National Bureau Of Economic Research, which analyzed household wealth trends in the United States from 1962 to 2016, the top 20% of wealthiest households received nine out of ten slices (90% of the pie). Alarmingly, almost half of these nine slices (40% of the entire pie) were claimed by the richest 1% alone.

In contrast, the middle and upper-middle classes were left to share a single slice, equivalent to roughly 10% of the total wealth. The lower middle class received mere crumbs, representing a meager 0.3% of the total wealth. Most strikingly, the bottom 20% of Americans, those most impoverished, received nothing at all. In fact, their slice is more accurately represented as a negative space, as they are, on average, in debt by over $6,000.

This visual demonstration paints a grim picture of America's economic disparity. The wealth chasm in the country continues to deepen, with no signs of slowing down. The steadily expanding economy and historically low unemployment rates may present an illusion of prosperity, but beneath this veneer, the stark reality is that American families exist in vastly divergent financial circumstances.

This profound inequality underscores a systemic issue that extends beyond simple economics — it influences access to opportunities, education, healthcare, and other critical resources, perpetuating a cycle of poverty that is increasingly difficult to escape. It's not just about wealth; it's about life chances, social mobility, and the very fabric of American society.

A: Chapter 6 explores the harsh reality of wealth inequality in the United States, presenting a thought-provoking analogy using a pie to depict the distribution of wealth. By using this relatable visual representation, the chapter effectively communicates the magnitude of the disparities that exist and highlights the systemic nature of the issue.

The chapter draws on a study by the National Bureau of Economic Research, revealing that a significant portion of the nation's wealth is concentrated in the hands of a small percentage of the population. The wealthiest 20% of households claim the majority of the pie, with the richest 1% alone holding a substantial share. In contrast, the middle and upper-middle classes are left with a meager slice, and the lower middle class receives a small fraction. Most strikingly, the bottom 20% of Americans, those in poverty, receive no slice at all, symbolizing their lack of wealth and financial struggle.

By presenting this portrayal of wealth distribution, the chapter highlights the severity of economic disparities in the country. It challenges the notion that prosperity is widely shared, emphasizing the significant divergences in financial circumstances that exist beneath the surface. It underscores the broader implications of wealth inequality, affecting access to opportunities, social mobility, and the overall fabric of society.

The chapter recognizes that wealth inequality is not solely an economic issue but a deeply ingrained systemic problem. It perpetuates a cycle of poverty and limited upward mobility, hindering individuals' access to essential resources such as education and healthcare. It underscores the need for comprehensive and targeted measures to address the root causes of wealth inequality and create a more equitable society.

By bringing attention to the stark reality of wealth inequality, the chapter prompts critical reflection on the structural factors that contribute to the unequal distribution of wealth. It encourages policymakers, researchers, and individuals to consider innovative solutions and policy interventions aimed at reducing economic disparities, promoting equal opportunities, and fostering a more inclusive society where everyone has a fair chance to succeed and thrive.

4: Chapter 6 makes a poignant and impactful presentation on the alarming levels of wealth inequality in the United States, by using the simple, universally understood analogy of a pie. This strong visual tool offers a striking representation of the country's wealth distribution, making it both accessible and relatable.

The chapter uses data from a study by the National Bureau Of Economic Research, which paints a dire picture: the richest 20% of households own 90% of the wealth. The distribution gets even more skewed when you consider that the richest 1% alone claim almost half of this share. This leaves the middle and upper-middle classes, the lower middle class, and the poorest 20% with alarmingly diminishing shares of the wealth pie.

What is particularly striking in this analysis is the state of the bottom 20% of Americans. They do not merely receive no slice of the pie; they are actually represented as a negative space, signifying debt. This striking image brings home the crushing reality of poverty for many Americans.

The chapter notes that economic indicators such as growth and unemployment can mask this inequality, creating an illusion of prosperity. However, wealth inequality is not just a matter of economics; it deeply impacts the social fabric, affecting access to opportunities, education, healthcare, and other vital resources.

The commentary raises an essential point - wealth inequality perpetuates a poverty cycle that is increasingly hard to break. It is a systemic issue that needs to be addressed to ensure a more equitable society. The growing wealth gap is not just about money but also about social mobility and the life chances of millions of Americans.

The stark reality of wealth inequality calls for structural interventions and innovative solutions to promote equal opportunities, reduce economic disparities, and foster an inclusive society. By highlighting the systemic nature of this issue, the chapter underscores the urgent need to engage with wealth inequality not as an abstract economic problem, but as a critical social issue that impacts the lives and futures of real people. This narrative encourages us to reimagine our approach towards achieving a fair and just society.

Chapter 7

Unveiling the Economic Perils of Billionaire Boom: The Drive Towards Inequality

W: A striking paradox has begun to unfold across the globe; wealth accumulation for the ultra-rich intensifies, while a vast population is plunged further into poverty. This stark contradiction is highlighted as global leaders assemble at the annual World Economic Forum in the picturesque Swiss town of Davos. It's a startling scenario: simultaneous surges in extreme wealth and severe poverty, a phenomenon not seen in the last quarter-century.

As the cost of basic necessities skyrockets, millions across the United States and beyond grapple with increasingly strained budgets. Meanwhile, the wealthiest 1% have almost doubled their wealth in comparison to the rest of the world in the past two years. This unsettling trend forms the core of our recent report, "Survival of the Richest", which scrutinizes the troubling escalation in billionaire wealth since 2020 and the subsequent deepening of poverty.

Simply put, the concentration of wealth in the hands of a few is detrimental to the economy. The report outlines five key reasons for this:

1. **Unprecedented Concentration of Wealth:** Since 2020, the uppermost 1% have amassed nearly two-thirds of all newly generated wealth. Their daily income stands at a staggering $2.7 billion, six times the combined income of the bottom 90% of humanity. This chasm of wealth not only exacerbates poverty but also aggravates gender inequality and hinders climate change mitigation. The escalating concentration of wealth undermines efforts towards poverty eradication and marks the first increase in global inequality in decades. As a consequence, the World Bank predicted in 2022 that the U.N.'s goal to eliminate poverty by 2030 is unlikely to be achieved.

2. **An Inequitable Tax System:** The ultra-wealthy enjoy alarmingly low tax rates, around 3%, while professionals like teachers and nurses pay significantly more. If we were to implement a 2-3% wealth tax rate on multi-millionaires and a 5% rate on billionaires globally, it would raise approximately $1.7 trillion annually. These funds could bolster underfunded social programs, environmental initiatives, and

economic plans, thereby alleviating burdens like healthcare and childcare costs. Implementing such tax rates could potentially lift 2 billion people out of poverty, a crucial step towards reducing inequality.

3. **A Simultaneous Rise in Extreme Wealth and Poverty:** As inflation soars worldwide, workers struggle to meet their basic needs, such as food and bills. Corporations inflate the prices of goods not out of necessity but to maximize shareholders' dividends, augmenting the wealth of the ultra-rich while propelling more people into poverty. Last year, 95 food and energy corporations doubled their profits, funnelling $257 billion to already wealthy shareholders, instead of investing in their workforce. Amidst such corporate greed, 1.7 billion workers live in nations where inflation exceeds wage growth.

4. **The Unbalanced Impact of the Pandemic:** American billionaires saw their wealth grow by 33% since the onset of the pandemic, even as the country experienced its worst economic growth since World War II. While marginalized groups bore the brunt of this economic downturn, the top 1% expanded their wealth significantly. This imbalance is

symptomatic of a system that has long been skewed to favor the wealthy, with labor laws, CEO compensations, and privatization of public assets all rigged to perpetuate the wealth of the rich, leaving little safeguard for the average individual.

5. **The Carbon Footprint of the Wealthy:** The world's richest individuals contribute a million times more carbon to the atmosphere than the average person, exacerbating climate change. About 125 of the world's wealthiest individuals are deeply invested in polluting industries, cumulatively releasing an average of 3 million tons of carbon per year. Their continued support for fossil fuels remains steadfast, irrespective of the dire consequences suffered by the rest of the world due to climate change. Severe hurricanes, flash floods, and wildfires, all products of climate change, pose a growing threat to populations worldwide.

The escalating levels of global inequality are alarming, to say the least. It's high time that we implemented policies that disrupt the perpetuation of this billionaire boom. Oxfam champions a comprehensive increase in the taxation of the super-rich, urging governments worldwide to levy substantial taxes on multi-millionaires and billionaires. This, they argue, is a critical move towards redistributing wealth, tackling inequality, and creating a fairer world for all.

A: Chapter 7 delves into the economic perils of the billionaire boom and provides a critical analysis of the factors driving wealth inequality. The chapter highlights the concerning trend of extreme wealth accumulation among the top 1% while poverty levels continue to worsen for a significant portion of the population.

One notable aspect discussed in the chapter is the unprecedented concentration of wealth in recent years. This concentration not only exacerbates poverty but also perpetuates gender inequality and hinders efforts to address climate change. It is important to recognize that extreme wealth disparities can have far-reaching consequences beyond economic disparities, impacting social cohesion, political stability, and overall societal well-being.

The chapter also sheds light on the inequitable tax systems that contribute to wealth inequality. The ultra-wealthy often benefit from preferential tax treatment, paying significantly lower tax rates compared to middle-class workers. Implementing progressive tax policies, particularly on multi-millionaires and billionaires, can help address this disparity and provide additional resources for social programs, infrastructure development, and poverty alleviation efforts.

Furthermore, the simultaneous rise in extreme wealth and poverty during a period of global inflation is a concerning issue discussed in the chapter. It highlights how corporations prioritize profit maximization by inflating prices, leaving workers struggling to afford basic necessities. This practice further widens the wealth gap and creates economic hardships for vulnerable populations. Policies that promote fair wages, labor rights, and consumer protections are crucial in addressing this imbalance and ensuring a more equitable distribution of resources.

The chapter also underscores the unbalanced impact of the pandemic on wealth distribution. While marginalized groups faced economic hardships and job losses, billionaires experienced significant wealth growth. This highlights the systemic biases and structural inequalities that favor the wealthy and leave the most vulnerable populations at a disadvantage during times of crisis. Addressing these structural issues requires comprehensive reforms in areas such as labor laws, social safety nets, and wealth redistribution mechanisms.

Lastly, the chapter highlights the environmental impact of extreme wealth, particularly in relation to carbon emissions and climate change. Wealthy individuals, often heavily invested in polluting industries, contribute disproportionately to carbon emissions. This exacerbates the environmental challenges faced by the world while the consequences are felt disproportionately by marginalized communities and future generations. Sustainable economic policies and a transition to a low-carbon economy are essential to mitigate the environmental impact of extreme wealth and ensure a more sustainable and equitable future.

In conclusion, the chapter calls for comprehensive policy interventions to disrupt the billionaire boom and address the escalating levels of wealth inequality. It emphasizes the need for progressive taxation, fair labor practices, environmental sustainability, and robust social programs. By tackling wealth concentration and promoting equitable distribution of resources, societies can work towards a more inclusive and sustainable economic system that benefits all members of society.

4: Chapter 7 provides an in-depth exploration of the global trend towards escalating wealth inequality, specifically focusing on the substantial accumulation of wealth among the ultra-rich. It masterfully interweaves economic, social, and environmental perspectives to shed light on the complex, multifaceted nature of this issue.

The report "Survival of the Richest" is referenced as a key source in this chapter, highlighting alarming statistics, such as the top 1% amassing nearly two-thirds of all newly generated wealth since 2020, while the bottom 90% of humanity is barely scraping by. The chapter further reveals how this concentration of wealth inhibits progress in other areas like gender equality and climate change mitigation. This connection between wealth inequality and other societal challenges is a significant point that demonstrates the interdependent nature of global issues.

Chapter 7 also criticizes the current tax system, suggesting it is rigged in favor of the ultra-wealthy who enjoy significantly lower tax rates. It posits the potential of a global wealth tax as a tool for inequality reduction, a controversial proposal that has been a subject of heated debate among economists and policymakers. It argues that such a tax could raise funds necessary for social programs, environmental initiatives, and economic development, thus addressing both poverty and inequality.

The chapter also discusses the juxtaposition of extreme wealth and poverty amidst soaring inflation. It critiques corporations for prioritizing shareholder dividends over workforce investment and consumer affordability, exacerbating wealth disparity and creating precarious living conditions for many.

Furthermore, the chapter points out the stark contrast in how the pandemic has affected different economic groups, exacerbating pre-existing inequalities. This points towards the deep-seated structural imbalances in our economy, emphasizing the need for systemic changes.

Lastly, the chapter connects wealth inequality with climate change, detailing how the carbon footprint of the wealthy significantly exceeds that of the average person, thus linking environmental degradation to economic disparity. This contributes to an emerging discourse about the intersection of economic and environmental justice.

Chapter 7 underlines the urgent need for international policies aimed at disrupting the growth of billionaire wealth and fostering a more equitable global economy. By painting a comprehensive picture of the drivers and impacts of wealth inequality, the chapter puts forth a compelling case for far-reaching systemic reforms. It emphasizes that addressing wealth inequality is not merely an issue of economic justice but is central to social equity, environmental sustainability, and overall societal well-being.

Chapter 8

Unmasking the Political Power Play of Billionaires: Global Implications and Repercussions

W: The current global scenario underscores a universal trend: the rise of billionaires in political arenas, an occurrence transcending national boundaries from Austria to Australia, Russia to the United Kingdom. The ascent of these financially robust individuals to political prominence has given rise to the term "oligarchs" in Russia, and "princelings" in China. This wealthy tycoon-led political involvement is not just limited to these nations but is increasingly commonplace worldwide. This intertwining of extreme wealth and politics raises critical questions about undue influence and fairness in democratic processes.

The involvement of billionaires in political discourse and policy-making isn't a novel phenomenon. In "Billionaires and Stealth Politics" (Page, Seawright, & Lacombe, 2018), the authors elaborate on how the wealthiest individuals in the United States exert substantial influence on American politics, often behind the scenes. Similarly, "Capital without

Borders" (Harrington, 2016) explores how wealth managers impact policy and help billionaires navigate around legislation, reinforcing the notion that wealth can indirectly manipulate legal and political structures.

Chapter 9 delves into the profound implications of the Tax Cuts and Jobs Act (TCJA) of 2017, enacted during President Trump's administration. The TCJA, touted as the most substantial tax reform since 1986, unsurprisingly had significant socio-economic implications. The chapter not only explores the disparities created by these changes but also points towards the less visible yet potent hand of billionaire influence on such legislations.

This influence, although hard to quantify or prove explicitly, leaves noticeable trails in the policy-making process. The TCJA brought about considerable tax breaks for the wealthiest segment of society and corporations, with minor benefits trickling down to middle and low-income families. The tax overhaul resulted in a lower tax burden for those earning more than $200,000, while the benefits were far less significant for those earning less. Similarly, corporations experienced a substantial tax cut, which inevitably led to an increase in the refunds they received.

These trends suggest that the TCJA was, in fact, geared towards the interests of the richest individuals and corporations. Wealthy entities have been known to leverage their resources to shape public policies to their favor, often through campaign financing, lobbying, and funding think-tanks. Thus, the contours of the TCJA raise the plausible question about the extent of the billionaires' influence over the legislation, although the discrete nature of these influences makes it challenging to establish a direct causality.

This chapter invites readers to reflect on how such policy outcomes, arguably skewed in favor of the wealthiest, pose a fundamental challenge to the core democratic principles of equality and fairness. It underscores the necessity of maintaining a political system that operates for the betterment of all its constituents, not just the ultra-rich.

The billionaire influence, if unchecked, can have the potential to undermine the democratic ethos of a society. Hence, acknowledging this influence becomes the first step towards crafting policies that guard against such undemocratic skewing of legislation. The aim should be to work towards a more balanced, transparent political system that stands for the interests of everyone and not just caters to the affluent few.

By casting light on the potential distortions caused by wealth in policy-making, the chapter calls for a re-evaluation of how democracies operate. It emphasizes the need for robust safeguards to prevent undue influence from subverting the democratic process and underscores the significance of reforms that can deliver a fairer and more equitable socio-economic landscape. This chapter urges a call to action for all stakeholders to ensure that the democratic process is genuinely representative and works in favor of the many, not just the few.

As a system, democracy prides itself on equality and fairness. However, the infiltration of this level of wealth into politics threatens these principles. The concern is not unfounded, given the historical tendency for those with excessive wealth to use their resources to influence policy and legal systems, often in their favor (Piketty, 2014).

Wealth in politics not only contributes to increased inequality but also hampers social development. A study by Gilens & Page (2014) suggested that policy changes in the U.S. are strongly influenced by economic elites and business-centered interest groups, potentially undermining the public interest. The impact of this billionaire-led political involvement transcends national boundaries, shaping global policies and economic dynamics.

Acknowledging these risks, the discourse needs to focus on how to maintain a balanced policy-making process. It is imperative to discuss safeguards that ensure the wealthiest do not have disproportionate influence. Policies such as limiting campaign contributions, imposing stricter regulations on lobbying, and reinforcing the transparency of political funding could help mitigate the potential abuse of power (Scheiber, 2018).

Our goal is to illuminate the potential dangers of concentrated power and propose ways to ensure governance benefits all citizens, not just the privileged few. This approach necessitates an ongoing commitment to scrutinizing political contributions and influence, keeping democratic processes accessible, and truly representative.

A: Chapter 8 delves into the complex issue of the political power wielded by billionaires and its global implications. The chapter highlights the increasing involvement of wealthy individuals in political arenas worldwide, raising concerns about the fairness and integrity of democratic processes.

The chapter acknowledges that billionaires' involvement in politics is not a new phenomenon and references previous studies that have explored the influence of wealth on political systems. These studies shed light on how the wealthiest individuals can exert significant behind-the-scenes influence on policy-making, and how wealth managers help navigate legal and political structures to benefit billionaires' interests. This intertwining of extreme wealth and politics calls into question the principles of equality and fairness that underpin democratic systems.

One of the key concerns raised in the chapter is the potential for billionaires' political involvement to exacerbate inequality and hinder social development. The influence of economic elites and business-centered interest groups on policy changes can undermine the public interest and result in policies that primarily benefit the wealthy. This influence extends beyond national boundaries, shaping global policies and economic dynamics.

To address these risks and maintain a balanced policy-making process, the chapter suggests implementing safeguards to prevent disproportionate influence by the wealthiest individuals. Measures such as limiting campaign contributions, imposing stricter regulations on lobbying, and increasing transparency in political funding are proposed as potential solutions. These measures aim to mitigate the potential abuse of power and ensure that governance serves the interests of all citizens, not just the privileged few.

The chapter emphasizes the importance of ongoing scrutiny of political contributions and influence to uphold the principles of democracy. By keeping democratic processes accessible, transparent, and representative, societies can strive for a more equitable and inclusive political system.

In conclusion, the chapter sheds light on the potential dangers associated with the concentration of political power in the hands of billionaires. It calls for a critical examination of the role of wealth in politics and the implementation of measures to safeguard democratic processes. By addressing these concerns, societies can work towards a political system that upholds equality, fairness, and the well-being of all citizens.

4: Chapter 8 delves into a phenomenon that is globally evident but not often openly discussed: the intersection of enormous wealth and political power. It underscores how billionaires, irrespective of geographic location, are leveraging their wealth to exert considerable influence over political landscapes, a trend raising substantial concerns about the implications for democracy and fairness.

The chapter references important studies such as "Billionaires and Stealth Politics" and "Capital without Borders," which shed light on how the ultra-wealthy, in the United States and elsewhere, are able to mold political narratives and policies to serve their interests. Such influence is often exerted discreetly, making it all the more dangerous as it largely escapes public scrutiny.

Moreover, the chapter draws on Piketty's work to express concern over the historical precedent of wealth being used to manipulate legal and political structures, often to the detriment of the broader population. This brings to light a paradox within democracies: while such systems are supposed to champion equality and fairness, the infiltration of extreme wealth can erode these very principles.

A critical aspect this chapter brings forth is the connection between wealth in politics and increased societal inequality and stunted social development. It points to the research by Gilens & Page, which implies that economic elites and interest groups have a substantial bearing on policy changes. This observation suggests that political decisions, instead of addressing public needs, are often skewed to cater to the desires of the wealthy.

Given the risks involved, the chapter underscores the necessity for implementing safeguards that prevent the ultra-wealthy from having a disproportionate influence on politics. It recommends limiting campaign contributions, stricter regulation of lobbying, and enhancing transparency in political funding, as potential measures to ensure the equitable functioning of democracies.

The core message of Chapter 8 revolves around the need for vigilance in monitoring political contributions and influence, especially from the extremely wealthy. It underscores the urgency of ensuring that governance and political decisions are taken with the welfare of all citizens in mind, not just the privileged few.

In conclusion, this chapter unravels the intricate dynamics of wealth and politics, emphasizing the need for countermeasures to prevent the distortion of democratic processes. By fostering transparency and implementing appropriate checks and balances, societies can move towards a political system that truly upholds the democratic principles of equality and fairness.

Chapter 9

Trump's Tax Cuts and the Invisible Hand of Billionaire Influence

W: The Tax Cuts and Jobs Act (TCJA) of 2017, implemented during President Trump's tenure, marked the most significant U.S. tax reform since 1986. Central to this reform were substantial changes favoring corporations and high-income individuals. The implications of the TCJA extend beyond the domain of fiscal policy, touching upon issues of socio-economic inequality and the role of billionaire influence in shaping legislation.

The TCJA brought significant changes, particularly for higher-income Americans. Income tax rates across various brackets decreased, with corporations seeing a drop in tax rates from 35% to 21%. In the personal realm, the standard deduction was nearly doubled from $6,350 in 2017 to $12,000 in 2018, while the child tax credit also increased from $1,000 to $2,000. However, some itemized deductions saw limitation or elimination. The outcomes were not uniformly distributed across income brackets, with most savings seen by high-income families. Middle-class families had mixed results, while low-income families reaped the least benefits.

A closer look at the numbers reveals that taxpayers with an adjusted gross income (AGI) of at least $200,000 saw the most substantial increase in their refunds. Conversely, those with an AGI below $100,000 paid less income tax overall, but those just above this threshold (many of whom would be middle-class families) owed more tax on average. Between 2017 and 2018, corporations paid 22.4% less income tax. The total value of refunds issued by the IRS to businesses also increased by 33.8%.

Given the significant benefits accruing to corporations and high-income individuals, questions arise regarding the influence of billionaires and the ultra-wealthy on the creation and passage of the TCJA. Wealthy individuals and corporations often have vested interests in policy outcomes, leading them to deploy their resources in political campaigns, lobbying, and think-tanks. The outcome of this influence, whether direct or indirect, is legislation that often works to preserve and augment their wealth.

The TCJA is a case in point. The reduction in corporate tax rates and the adjustment of personal income tax brackets—particularly the reductions in the capital gains tax rates—bear the hallmarks of a policy beneficial for the ultra-wealthy, particularly those with significant corporate and investment interests.

Determining direct causality between billionaire influence and specific pieces of legislation like the TCJA is challenging due to the covert nature of this influence. However, the lopsided benefit distribution of the TCJA favoring the wealthy provides circumstantial evidence of billionaire influence in its design and implementation.

Such influence, if it exists, represents a challenge to democratic principles of fairness, equality, and government of the people, by the people, and for the people. Acknowledging this influence is the first step towards formulating policy safeguards and reforms that ensure a fair, transparent, and balanced political system that works for everyone, not just the wealthiest.

A: Chapter 9 delves into the Tax Cuts and Jobs Act (TCJA) of 2017 and its implications for socio-economic inequality, as well as the role of billionaire influence in shaping legislation. The TCJA brought significant changes to the U.S. tax system, favoring corporations and high-income individuals. This chapter raises questions about the distribution of benefits and the potential influence of billionaires in the creation and passage of the TCJA.

Examining the impact of the TCJA reveals that high-income individuals and corporations were the primary beneficiaries of the tax reform. While income tax rates decreased and certain deductions increased, the outcomes were not evenly distributed across income brackets. High-income families saw the most substantial increases in their refunds, while middle-class and low-income families experienced mixed results and limited benefits.

The numbers further highlight the disparities resulting from the TCJA. Taxpayers with higher adjusted gross income (AGI) experienced significant increases in their refunds, while those just above the middle-class threshold owed more tax on average. Corporations also benefited greatly, paying significantly less income tax, and the total value of refunds issued to businesses increased substantially.

These outcomes raise concerns about the influence of billionaires and the ultra-wealthy in shaping the TCJA. Wealthy individuals and corporations have the resources to deploy in political campaigns, lobbying efforts, and think-tanks, often pursuing policies that align with their own interests and contribute to preserving and augmenting their wealth.

While establishing direct causality between billionaire influence and specific legislation is challenging, the imbalanced distribution of benefits in the TCJA suggests the potential role of billionaire influence in its design and implementation. This underscores the need to critically examine the influence of wealth on policy outcomes and the potential implications for democratic principles.

Recognizing the influence of billionaires in policy-making is essential in formulating safeguards and reforms that promote fairness, equality, and transparency in the political system. Such measures can help ensure that legislation serves the interests of all citizens, not just the wealthiest few. By addressing the potential influence of billionaires, society can work towards a more equitable and inclusive democratic process that upholds the principles of government by the people and for the people.

4: Chapter 9 delves into the profound implications of the Tax Cuts and Jobs Act (TCJA) of 2017, enacted during President Trump's administration. The TCJA, touted as the most substantial tax reform since 1986, unsurprisingly had significant socio-economic implications. The chapter not only explores the disparities created by these changes but also points towards the less visible yet potent hand of billionaire influence on such legislations.

This influence, although hard to quantify or prove explicitly, leaves noticeable trails in the policy-making process. The TCJA brought about considerable tax breaks for the wealthiest segment of society and corporations, with minor benefits trickling down to middle and low-income families. The tax overhaul resulted in a lower tax burden for those earning more than $200,000, while the benefits were far less significant for those earning less. Similarly, corporations experienced a substantial tax cut, which inevitably led to an increase in the refunds they received.

These trends suggest that the TCJA was, in fact, geared towards the interests of the richest individuals and corporations. Wealthy entities have been known to leverage their resources to shape public policies to their favor, often through campaign financing, lobbying, and funding think-tanks. Thus, the contours of the TCJA raise the plausible question about the extent of the billionaires' influence over the legislation, although the discrete nature of these influences makes it challenging to establish a direct causality.

This chapter invites readers to reflect on how such policy outcomes, arguably skewed in favor of the wealthiest, pose a fundamental challenge to the core democratic principles of equality and fairness. It underscores the necessity of maintaining a political system that operates for the betterment of all its constituents, not just the ultra-rich.

The billionaire influence, if unchecked, can have the potential to undermine the democratic ethos of a society. Hence, acknowledging this influence becomes the first step towards crafting policies that guard against such undemocratic skewing of legislation. The aim should be to work towards a more balanced, transparent political system that stands for the interests of everyone and not just caters to the affluent few.

By casting light on the potential distortions caused by wealth in policy-making, the chapter calls for a re-evaluation of how democracies operate. It emphasizes the need for robust safeguards to prevent undue influence from subverting the democratic process and underscores the significance of reforms that can deliver a fairer and more equitable socio-economic landscape. This chapter urges a call to action for all stakeholders to ensure that the democratic process is genuinely representative and works in favor of the many, not just the few.

Chapter 10

The History of Taxation in the U.S.: Benefitting the Wealthy?

W: Over the past half-century, the United States has seen a substantial shift in its taxation system, one that has often favored the wealthiest of the society. The link between tax laws, the economy, and the wealthy has been a complex interplay, highly debated amongst economists and policymakers.

The U.S. did not start levying income tax on its citizens, particularly the wealthy, until the 1910s. Post-World War II and into the 1950s, the highest income tax bracket was over 90 percent. However, as the decades passed, those in the highest tax bracket experienced a significant decrease in the tax rate, particularly under the administrations of Ronald Reagan and George W. Bush.

President Reagan and President Bush both subscribed to supply-side economics, positing that reducing the tax rates for the highest earners would spur economic growth. However, the historical record presents a complex picture.

The Reagan administration's tax cuts in the early 1980s did coincide with a period of economic growth. However, when Bush enacted a series of tax cuts in 2001 and 2003, the economy stumbled and eventually led to the Great Recession. This suggests that tax cuts for the rich do not necessarily lead to economic prosperity and might even lead to economic instability.

A 2012 paper published by the Congressional Research Service concluded that there was no correlation between top tax rates and economic growth. This finding was met with resistance from Congressional Republicans, who argued that the study did not account for the long-term benefits of tax rate cuts.

President John F. Kennedy and President Lyndon B. Johnson also implemented tax cuts in the 1960s in hopes of economic growth. They reduced the top tax rate to 70%, which coincided with a period of increased GDP growth per capita. This was also true for President Clinton, who increased the top marginal tax rate to 39.6% in the 1990s, which was followed by above-average economic growth.

Under President George W. Bush, tax cuts in 2001 and 2003 dropped the top tax rate to 35%. These cuts, which were set to expire in 10 years, were followed by an economic decline, which culminated in the 2008 financial crisis. In contrast, under President Obama, who returned the top marginal rate to 39.6% from the Clinton era, the economy posted below-average growth, but it did not plunge into recession as it did under President Bush.

The most recent proposal under President Trump suggests a return to the policy of tax cuts for the wealthy, with plans to reduce the number of tax brackets and lower the top marginal tax rate to 35%.

Historically, tax cuts for the wealthy have been justified as a means to spur economic growth. However, the economic outcomes following such cuts have been varied and unpredictable. There is no guarantee that reducing the tax burden for the wealthy results in economic prosperity. More often than not, these tax cuts tend to disproportionately benefit the wealthiest individuals, contributing to increased wealth inequality.

While the ideal tax rate and structure continues to be a topic of intense debate, it is clear from history that taxation policies can have profound implications on wealth distribution and the health of the economy. It is crucial that policymakers take into account this historical context and consider the broader societal impact when crafting new tax laws.

A: The history of taxation in the United States reveals a complex relationship between tax laws, the economy, and the wealthy. Over the years, there have been significant shifts in tax rates, particularly for the highest earners, leading to debates among economists and policymakers about the impact of these changes.

The implementation of income tax on wealthy citizens in the 1910s marked a significant shift in tax policy. In subsequent decades, the highest income tax brackets experienced a considerable decrease in tax rates, particularly during the Reagan and George W. Bush administrations. These administrations subscribed to supply-side economics, arguing that lower tax rates for the wealthy would stimulate economic growth.

The historical record, however, paints a more nuanced picture. While Reagan's tax cuts coincided with a period of economic growth in the 1980s, the tax cuts implemented by President Bush in 2001 and 2003 were followed by economic instability and the Great Recession. This suggests that the relationship between tax cuts for the rich and economic prosperity is not straightforward, and other factors come into play.

A 2012 study by the Congressional Research Service found no correlation between top tax rates and economic growth. However, there were arguments against this conclusion, claiming that the study did not consider the long-term benefits of tax rate cuts.

Examining specific historical cases further adds complexity to the relationship between tax rates and economic outcomes. Presidents Kennedy and

Johnson implemented tax cuts in the 1960s, which coincided with increased GDP growth per capita. President Clinton's increase in the top marginal tax rate in the 1990s was followed by above-average economic growth. On the other hand, President Bush's tax cuts in the early 2000s were associated with an economic decline and the 2008 financial crisis. President Obama's restoration of higher tax rates did not lead to recession but saw below-average economic growth.

The recent proposal under President Trump to reduce tax rates for the wealthy reflects a return to the policy of tax cuts. However, the historical record demonstrates that the outcomes of such cuts are unpredictable, and they often contribute to increased wealth inequality.

While debates about the ideal tax rate and structure persist, it is essential for policymakers to consider the historical context and broader societal implications when crafting tax laws. The goal should be to ensure a fair distribution of the tax burden and to promote economic stability and growth for all members of society, rather than disproportionately benefiting the wealthiest individuals. A thorough understanding of the historical outcomes of tax policies can inform more informed and equitable decision-making in the future.

4: The history of taxation in the U.S. is a prime example of the power dynamics in economic policy making. Over the past century, we've seen tax policies oscillating, largely influenced by the prevailing political climate and economic theories of the time. More often than not, these policy decisions have disproportionately benefited the wealthy, exacerbating wealth inequality.

In the early 20th century, the introduction of income tax was seen as a tool to ensure wealthier citizens contributed proportionately to the country's fiscal needs. This progressive approach to taxation reached its peak in the 1950s, with the highest income tax bracket reaching over 90%. The core principle here was a graduated tax rate which asked those with the most means to contribute the most.

However, the latter half of the 20th century marked a shift in taxation policy under the influence of supply-side economics, championed by Presidents Reagan and Bush. This theory held that decreasing tax rates for high earners would stimulate economic activity, benefiting society at large. Yet, the historical record seems to contradict this notion, suggesting a more complicated relationship between tax rates and economic prosperity.

For instance, while Reagan's tax cuts in the 1980s were followed by economic growth, Bush's tax cuts in the early 2000s coincided with economic turbulence and the Great Recession. These examples illustrate that while tax cuts can provide short-term economic boosts, they may also lead to longer-term economic instability, and do not necessarily spur sustained growth.

Moreover, the assumption that tax cuts for the rich automatically benefit the broader economy is contentious. A Congressional Research Service paper from 2012 suggests there's no correlation between top tax rates and economic growth, challenging the underlying principle of supply-side economics. However, this study faced pushback from those who still argue for the long-term benefits of tax cuts.

Tax cuts implemented by Kennedy and Johnson in the 1960s, and tax increases under Clinton in the 1990s, both led to periods of robust economic growth. This further underlines the intricate relationship between tax rates and economic prosperity, suggesting other factors play significant roles in shaping economic outcomes.

Tax policies under recent presidents continue this contentious pattern. President Bush's tax cuts led to an economic decline, culminating in the 2008 financial crisis, while under President Obama, despite returning to higher top marginal tax rates, the economy posted slow but steady growth.

The proposal by President Trump to reduce the number of tax brackets and lower the top marginal tax rate to 35% continued the trend towards tax cuts for the wealthy. Yet, history suggests such measures may not guarantee economic prosperity and, in fact, might contribute to increasing wealth inequality.

Thus, the history of taxation in the U.S. underscores the need for a more nuanced understanding of how tax laws interact with the economy. Policymakers need to consider not just the short-term impacts, but also long-term societal consequences, particularly on wealth distribution and economic health. Efforts to simplify this complex issue into easy-to-digest political talking points often serve to obscure the nuanced realities of how tax policy impacts the economy and wealth inequality.

Chapter 11

Addressing Regressivity in the American Tax Code

Introduction

W: The American tax code has undergone significant changes in recent decades, resulting in a slide toward regressivity. This chapter explores the need to reverse this trend and discusses the implications of decreasing top marginal income tax rates and regressive state and local taxes. It highlights the unequal treatment of income from ownership versus income from salaries and wages, and the overall impact on income inequality. By addressing regressivity in the tax code, a more equitable and progressive system can be established.

Decline in Top Marginal Income Tax Rates

The top marginal income tax rates in the United States have experienced a significant decline over the years. In the early 1950s, the top marginal tax rate stood at 92%, while it currently stands at 37%. This shift has primarily benefited the highest-income earners in society. The reduction in top marginal rates has implications for income inequality and wealth accumulation, as it rewards wealth over work.

Income Tax Bias: Wealth versus Work

One of the key issues in the American tax code is the differential treatment of income from ownership and income from salaries and wages. Income from ownership, such as capital gains and dividends, is taxed at significantly lower rates compared to income earned through work. This bias in favor of wealth contributes to the growing wealth gap and exacerbates income inequality. The tax code should be revised to ensure a fairer treatment of all sources of income.

Regressivity of State and Local Taxes

While federal income taxes have become less progressive, state and local taxes often exhibit regressive patterns. Regressive taxes disproportionately affect lower-income individuals and families, as they tend to consume a higher percentage of their income. Sales taxes, property taxes, and other forms of taxation contribute to the regressive nature of the overall tax system. Addressing these regressive elements is crucial to promoting fairness and reducing income disparities.

Progressivity and the Middle Class

The current tax code offers some progressivity for individuals between the poor and the upper-middle class. However, the tax rates for the very rich actually decrease, further exacerbating income inequality. To achieve a more equitable system, it is necessary to ensure that tax rates remain progressive even for the highest-income earners. This will help mitigate the growing wealth gap and promote a fairer distribution of resources.

Conclusion

The regressive nature of the American tax code calls for a shift toward progressivity and fairness. Reversing the slide toward regressivity requires addressing multiple aspects, including the decline in top marginal income tax rates, the bias in favor of income from ownership, and the regressive nature of state and local taxes. By implementing reforms that promote a more equitable distribution of the tax burden, the tax code can play a crucial role in reducing income inequality and fostering a more just society.

A: The regressive nature of the American tax code is a pressing issue that requires attention and reform. The decline in top marginal income tax rates over the years has contributed to a system that disproportionately benefits the highest-income earners. This shift in tax rates has implications for income inequality, as it rewards wealth accumulation over work. Reversing this trend and establishing a more progressive tax system is crucial for promoting economic fairness and reducing income disparities.

Another aspect that exacerbates regressivity in the tax code is the differential treatment of income from ownership and income from salaries and wages. Income from ownership, such as capital gains and dividends, is taxed at lower rates compared to income earned through work. This bias in favor of wealth contributes to the growing wealth gap and widens income inequality. It is essential to revise the tax code to ensure a fairer treatment of all sources of income, promoting equal opportunities and reducing wealth disparities.

In addition to federal income taxes, state and local taxes also play a role in the overall regressivity of the tax system. Many state and local taxes, such as sales taxes and property taxes, tend to be regressive, disproportionately burdening lower-income individuals and families. This regressive pattern further exacerbates income inequality and poses challenges to economic mobility. Addressing these regressive elements in state and local tax systems is crucial for promoting fairness and reducing the burden on lower-income households.

While the current tax code offers some progressivity for individuals between the poor and the upper-middle class, it falls short when it comes to the very wealthy. In fact, tax rates for the highest-income earners often decrease, contributing to the widening wealth gap. To create a more equitable system, it is necessary to ensure that tax rates remain progressive even for the wealthiest individuals. This can help mitigate the growing wealth disparities and promote a fairer distribution of resources in society.

In conclusion, addressing the regressivity in the American tax code requires comprehensive reforms that tackle multiple aspects, including the decline in top marginal tax rates, the bias toward income from ownership, and the regressive nature of state and local taxes. By implementing progressive tax policies and promoting fairness, the tax code can play a pivotal role in reducing income inequality and fostering a more just and equitable society. Such reforms are necessary to ensure that the tax system aligns with the principles of fairness, economic mobility, and social cohesion.

4: The U.S. tax code has seen significant changes over time, with an increasing trend towards regressivity, a system where the tax burden disproportionately falls on those with less income. This has profound implications for income inequality and the wealth gap in society. Addressing this issue requires a multi-faceted approach that includes revising the top marginal tax rates, rebalancing the treatment of income from wealth and work, and reforming state and local taxes.

Over the decades, the top marginal tax rates have seen a drastic decrease from 92% in the 1950s to 37% in the present day. While this reduction might stimulate economic activity and growth to an extent, it primarily benefits the highest income earners, leaving the middle and lower-income earners shouldering a disproportionate tax burden. This situation runs counter to the principle of progressive taxation where those who have more should contribute more. It is also worth noting that lower tax rates for high-income earners can further amplify wealth accumulation among the richest, exacerbating wealth inequality. Hence, revisiting top marginal tax rates should be a priority in tax reform.

A key discrepancy in the American tax code lies in the treatment of income from ownership and income from labor. The former, comprising of capital gains and dividends, is taxed at a significantly lower rate than income from work, such as wages and salaries. This bias can accelerate wealth accumulation among those who already own assets, thereby exacerbating the wealth gap. Addressing this discrepancy requires equalizing the tax treatment of all forms of income, which can help foster a more balanced and equitable tax system.

State and local taxes also contribute to the regressive nature of the U.S. tax system. These taxes often disproportionately affect low-income individuals who spend a larger percentage of their income on goods and services. Sales taxes, property taxes, and other forms of local taxes could be particularly burdensome for these populations, which points to a need for reform at the state and local levels to alleviate the tax burden on low-income households.

While the current tax code does display some progressivity, with those in the middle-income brackets generally bearing a larger tax burden relative to their income than the poor, this progressivity is not extended to the top of the income distribution. In fact, the very rich often face decreasing tax rates, which only intensifies income inequality. To ensure a more equitable system, it is crucial to extend progressivity to the highest income brackets as well.

In sum, to address the regressivity in the American tax code and the consequent wealth and income inequality, comprehensive reforms are necessary. These reforms should involve recalibrating top marginal tax rates, revising the unequal tax treatment of different types of income, and reconsidering the structure of state and local taxes. Such an overhaul can help foster a more equitable and just society where the tax burden is fairly distributed, reducing income inequality and promoting a healthier economy. This endeavor is critical in realigning the American tax system with the fundamental principles of fairness, opportunity, and equity.

Chapter 12

The Role of Labor Unions in Improving Workers' Pay

Introduction

W: Labor unions have played a crucial role in advocating for workers' rights and improving their pay and working conditions. This chapter explores the history of labor unions in the United States and discusses their significance in enhancing workers' wages. Despite a decline in union membership over the years, unions continue to have a substantial impact on economic inequality and serve as political and social forces in advocating for workers' interests.

History of Labor Unions in the United States

Labor unions in the United States have a rich history dating back to the late 18th century. They emerged as a response to the poor working conditions, long hours, and low wages that characterized the early industrial era. The formation of unions allowed workers to collectively bargain with employers, leading to the establishment of better working conditions, fair wages, and improved benefits. Key milestones in labor union history include the founding of the American Federation of Labor (AFL) in 1886 and the passage of landmark labor legislation such as the National Labor Relations Act (NLRA) in 1935.

Union Membership and Influence

While union membership has declined in recent decades, labor unions remain a significant force in the United States, particularly in the public sector. Despite representing a smaller percentage of the workforce, unions continue to advocate for workers' rights and mobilize their members around various social and political issues. Union workers tend to enjoy higher wages compared to their non-union counterparts, with studies showing an average pay advantage of 10-30% after controlling for relevant factors.

Impact on Economic Inequality

Research suggests a strong correlation between the decline of labor unions and rising income inequality in the United States. Labor unions historically have been effective in reducing economic inequality by negotiating for higher wages, benefits, and job security. Unionized workers tend to have better access to healthcare, retirement plans, and other benefits that contribute to a more equitable distribution of wealth. The decline in union membership has been associated with a decline in workers' bargaining power, leading to increased wage disparities.

Role in Advocacy and Social Issues

Labor unions have expanded their focus beyond traditional workplace issues and have become influential in advocating for broader social and political causes. Unions often collaborate with other activist organizations to address issues such as immigrant rights, environmental protections, healthcare reform, and living wage campaigns. Through collective action and political mobilization, unions have the ability to shape public policy and influence legislative decisions that impact workers' rights and economic well-being.

Conclusion

Labor unions have historically been instrumental in improving workers' pay and fighting for their rights. Despite challenges and declining membership, unions continue to play a vital role in advocating for fair wages, better working conditions, and reducing economic inequality. Their impact extends beyond the workplace, as unions actively engage in social and political advocacy on behalf of workers and marginalized communities. Recognizing the significance of labor unions in creating a more equitable society is essential for ensuring the well-being and prosperity of workers in the United States.

A: Labor unions have a long-standing history of advocating for workers' rights and improving their pay. They emerged as a response to the exploitative working conditions of the early industrial era, and their efforts have led to significant improvements in wages, benefits, and working conditions for workers across various industries. While union membership has experienced a decline in recent decades, the impact of labor unions on workers' pay remains substantial.

Labor unions have been influential in negotiating higher wages for their members through collective bargaining agreements. Studies have consistently shown that unionized workers tend to earn higher wages compared to non-union workers, even after controlling for relevant factors. The wage advantage of unionized workers can range from 10% to 30%, depending on the industry and occupation. This wage premium not only benefits union members directly but also sets higher standards for non-union employers, as they often need to compete with unionized firms to attract and retain skilled workers.

Beyond their impact on individual wages, labor unions also contribute to reducing economic inequality. The decline in union membership has coincided with a rise in income inequality in the United States. Research suggests that labor unions historically played a role in mitigating income disparities by negotiating for fair wages, benefits, and job security. Unionized workers tend to have better access to healthcare, retirement plans, and other essential benefits, which contribute to a more equitable distribution of wealth.

Labor unions also serve as powerful advocates for workers' rights and social issues. They have expanded their focus beyond workplace-related matters and actively engage in advocating for broader social and political causes. By collaborating with other organizations and participating in collective action, unions have the ability to influence public policy and shape legislative decisions that impact workers' rights and economic well-being. They often stand at the forefront of campaigns for immigrant rights, environmental protections, healthcare reform, and living wages, amplifying the voices of workers and marginalized communities.

Recognizing the significance of labor unions in creating a more equitable society is crucial. Their historical contributions to improving workers' pay, reducing inequality, and advocating for social justice are undeniable. As discussions around income disparities, workplace conditions, and workers' rights continue, the role of labor unions remains pivotal in promoting fair wages, enhancing working conditions, and ensuring the well-being and prosperity of workers in the United States.

4: Labor unions have been instrumental in shaping the landscape of workers' rights and pay in the United States. Since their inception in the late 18th century, unions have made significant strides in establishing fair wages, reasonable working hours, and better working conditions for workers. This has been possible primarily through the process of collective bargaining, a negotiation technique which has given workers a more level playing field against employers. Landmark events and legislations, such as the founding of the American Federation of Labor (AFL) and the passage of the National Labor Relations Act (NLRA), underscore the profound impact of unions on labor laws and workers' rights.

Union membership, however, has been declining over the years, reflecting changes in the economy, labor laws, and societal attitudes towards unions. Nonetheless, unions continue to exert influence in the workforce, particularly within the public sector. One of the key strengths of unions is their ability to negotiate higher wages for their members. Even though they now represent a smaller percentage of the workforce, research has shown that union workers generally earn more than their non-union counterparts, reflecting the tangible economic benefits of collective bargaining.

The decline in union membership has had broad implications for economic inequality. Unions have traditionally served as a counterbalance against the concentration of wealth and power, advocating for higher wages, better benefits, and job security for workers. They have been pivotal in ensuring that the fruits of economic growth are more equitably distributed. As union membership has decreased, there has been an erosion of workers' bargaining power, leading to stagnant wages for many and a growing income disparity.

Moreover, labor unions have evolved to become a significant political and social force. They have broadened their advocacy to encompass wider social and political issues, often aligning themselves with other activist groups. Their active involvement in issues such as immigrant rights, environmental protections, healthcare reform, and living wage campaigns demonstrates their commitment to social justice beyond just labor rights.

In conclusion, labor unions play a multifaceted role in advocating for workers' pay and rights. They serve as an economic equalizer, a political mobilizer, and a social advocate. Despite the challenges posed by declining membership and changes in the labor market, the work of unions remains vital in fighting for fair wages, decent working conditions, and a more equitable society. Looking ahead, it will be crucial to recognize and bolster the role of unions in pushing for greater economic equity and social justice.

Chapter 13

The Decline of Unions and its Impact on American Workers: A Discussion on "The Decline of Unions is Part of a Bad 50 Years for American Workers"
by Kevin Clarke

W: Introduction "The Decline of Unions and its Impact on American Workers" is a discussion based on the article "The Decline of Unions is Part of a Bad 50 Years for American Workers" written by Kevin Clarke. This article explores some of the factors contributing to the stagnant wages and growing wealth inequality in the United States, with a particular focus on the decline of organized labor and its impact on worker income and wealth distribution.

The Decline of Organized Labor As highlighted in Kevin Clarke's article, organized labor has witnessed a significant decline in membership, resulting in a weakened voice for workers and their rights. This decline has had far-reaching consequences for worker income and overall economic inequality.

Effects on Worker Income Clarke's analysis points out that despite the increasing productivity of workers, wages have remained stagnant, coinciding with the decline in union membership. The absence of organized labor has allowed upper management to claim a larger share of national income, further exacerbating income inequality and hindering workers' ability to secure higher wages and improved benefits.

- Impact on Wealth Distribution and Political Clout: The decline of unions and the concentration of wealth among the top echelons of society have resulted in outsized political influence, which perpetuates economic inequalities. Policies that favor the wealthy, such as tax breaks and anti-worker legislation, are often codified due to this influence. The push for right-to-work legislation, in particular, has weakened unions and diminished collective bargaining power, further eroding worker rights.

- Implications for Economic and Social Justice: As emphasized in the article and supported by Catholic social teaching, economic justice and the challenge of wealth inequality are crucial issues. The decline of unions not only hampers economic justice but also undermines the foundations of a just society. The concentration of wealth and the associated political clout perpetuate disparities and hinder efforts to create a more equitable and inclusive society.

Conclusion

"The Decline of Unions and its Impact on American Workers" highlights the important insights provided in Kevin Clarke's article, "The Decline of Unions is Part of a Bad 50 Years for American Workers." The decline of organized labor has had a significant impact on worker income, wealth distribution, and worker rights. To address these challenges and promote economic justice, it is crucial to reverse the erosion of labor unions and implement policies that prioritize fair wages, worker protections, and a more equitable distribution of wealth.

A: The decline of unions in the United States and its impact on American workers is a topic of significant concern and debate. Kevin Clarke's article sheds light on the factors contributing to this decline and the subsequent consequences for workers' income, wealth distribution, and overall economic inequality. Understanding the implications of this decline is essential for addressing the challenges faced by workers and striving for greater economic justice.

One of the key effects of the decline of organized labor is the stagnation of wages despite increased worker productivity. As unions lose their bargaining power and collective voice, workers face greater difficulty in securing higher wages and improved benefits. This has resulted in a disproportionate distribution of income, with a larger share going to upper management and corporate executives, while workers' wages remain stagnant. The growing gap between worker productivity and compensation exacerbates income inequality and hampers the economic well-being of workers.

Beyond income disparities, the decline of unions has also had implications for wealth distribution and political influence. With the concentration of wealth among the wealthiest individuals and corporations, there has been a corresponding increase in their political clout. This has enabled policies that favor the wealthy, such as tax breaks and anti-worker legislation, which further perpetuate economic inequalities. The ability of unions to mobilize workers and advocate for their rights has been diminished, weakening their influence in shaping policies that protect workers' interests.

The decline of unions not only has economic consequences but also poses challenges to social justice and a just society. Catholic social teaching, as highlighted in the article, recognizes the importance of economic justice and the need to address wealth inequality. The erosion of organized labor undermines the foundations of a just society by allowing the concentration of wealth and the associated political power to perpetuate disparities and hinder efforts to create a more equitable and inclusive society.

To address these challenges and promote economic and social justice, reversing the decline of unions is crucial. This involves empowering workers, strengthening their collective bargaining rights, and implementing policies that prioritize fair wages, worker protections, and a more equitable distribution of wealth. Recognizing the value of organized labor and its role in ensuring the well-being and rights of workers is essential for advancing the interests of workers, reducing economic inequalities, and building a more just society.

4: The decline of unions and its subsequent impact on American workers is indeed a multifaceted issue with profound implications. Drawing from Kevin Clarke's article and additional contextual knowledge, we can delve deeper into these implications, examining the historical context, the role of policy, and the potential for future reform.

Unions have traditionally served as a powerful force for worker rights, advocating for better wages, improved working conditions, and benefits. They gave workers a collective voice, allowing them to negotiate with employers on a more equal footing. However, over the past several decades, union membership has declined significantly. This decline is attributed to a myriad of factors including globalization, changes in labor laws, automation, and a shift towards a service-based economy.

The consequence of this decline is two-fold. First, it has resulted in wage stagnation despite increased worker productivity. As union power wanes, the balance of negotiation power tilts in favor of management and capital owners, resulting in a larger share of the income going to the top echelons. This contributes to rising income and wealth inequality, making it harder for workers to improve their economic status.

Second, the decline in union membership also means a decrease in the political clout of workers. As wealth concentrates at the top, so does political power. Wealthy individuals and corporations have more resources to lobby for legislation that favors their interests, often at the expense of workers. This dynamic leads to policies like tax cuts for the rich and anti-worker legislation such as right-to-work laws, which further weaken unions and contribute to income and wealth disparity.

From a perspective of economic and social justice, the weakening of unions is deeply concerning. As a vital tool for workers to exercise their rights and negotiate for fair wages and conditions, unions play a crucial role in ensuring a more equitable distribution of wealth and power. Their decline threatens the foundation of a just society, allowing wealth concentration and perpetuating socioeconomic disparities.

To reverse these adverse trends and promote economic justice, it's essential to prioritize policy reform aimed at strengthening unions and worker rights. This may include measures to protect the rights to unionize and collectively bargain, ensure fair wages, and address the influence of money in politics.

However, such reforms require a shift in the political landscape and public perception, recognizing the role of unions not only as protectors of workers but as key actors in maintaining economic balance and social justice. Through the lens of history, it becomes clear that the decline of unions is more than just a labor issue; it's a central factor contributing to the rise in income inequality and the erosion of the middle class. It underscores the need for comprehensive labor reform as part of the broader conversation about economic fairness and social justice.

Chapter 14

Erosion of Private-Sector Unions - Understanding the Intersection of Corporate Practices and Legal Changes

Introduction

W: The deterioration of worker bargaining power and collective bargaining has led to wage suppression and the erosion of labor's income share. These detrimental outcomes are increasingly apparent despite emerging policy proposals aimed at strengthening workers' ability to form unions. We see this trend in the broad reform of the National Labor Relations Act (NLRA) recently passed by the U.S. House of Representatives and the detailed proposals put forth by President-elect Joe Biden. The significance of such reforms stems from the acute need to understand the serious shortcomings in current law.

The Decline of Private-Sector Unionization

From the 1970s, we can observe a significant drop in private-sector unionization. It was a period marked by new unionization falling dramatically, a trend from which the labor movement has never fully recovered. Employers exploited structural weaknesses in labor law and successfully resisted efforts by workers to organize unions. The undercurrent of these movements is visible when analyzing the decrease in successful union elections and the initial collective bargaining agreement.

In the 1950s and 1960s, more than 1% of those employed participated in an NLRA election each year. However, by the 1980s, this figure had fallen to 0.29%. Workers began to lose elections at a higher rate, reflecting increased employer resistance. By the 1970s, workers were losing more than half of these elections. While 86% of workers who chose a union were able to win a first contract in the 1950s, that share declined to less than 70% in the 1970s and further slipped to 56% by the 1990s.

Employers' ability to defeat unions so effectively arose from a series of changes that tilted labor law heavily against workers and towards employers. While these employer-friendly laws existed as early as the 1940s, employers began to take full advantage of their power only from the 1970s.

Anti-Union Behavior and Legislative Stalemate

By the 1970s, employers were charged with committing significantly more unfair labor practices, such as firing union activists during organizing campaigns. They began to make extensive use of the "free speech" rights included in the Taft-Hartley amendments of 1947, holding mandatory "captive audience" meetings to voice opposition to unions. They also hired a growing "union avoidance" industry of consultants.

The law's ineffective remedies became clear, and the NLRB's attempts to hold employers accountable were stymied in the courts. Legislative efforts to strengthen the law in the 1960s, 1970s, and 1990s were thwarted by a united business community that opposed and defeated all attempts at legislative reform.

Underlying Causes and International Comparisons

Common arguments for the decline of unionization often cite globalization or automation as the driving forces. However, our empirical analysis suggests that at most one-fifth of the decline is due to manufacturing's erosion. We find severe declines in union coverage in nonmanufacturing sectors and industries as well. International comparisons of union decline also show a minor role for manufacturing decline, confirming our findings.

Recent survey research shows that nearly half of nonunion workers would vote to have union representation if given an opportunity. However, labor law has not kept pace with workers' interests and needs. Policymakers and stakeholders need to address these shortcomings if workers are to genuinely have the freedom to form and join unions.

In conclusion, a critical analysis of the erosion of workers' bargaining power, the impacts on today's workforce, and the need to strengthen the ability of workers to organize form the cornerstone of this chapter. The information presented here will provide necessary background and analysis to inform future policy discussions and decisions.

Globalization, Automation, and Union Decline

The decline in unionization has been frequently attributed to the impacts of globalization and automation. While it's true that these two factors have played a role in shaping labor markets, their impact on the decline in unionization has been overstated. Our data analysis shows that manufacturing's erosion could account for at most one-fifth of the decline in unionization. Notably, this decline is not exclusive to the manufacturing sector; it extends to non-manufacturing sectors such as utilities, transportation, construction, mining, and communications, and various industries like grocery stores, bus transportation, newspapers, metal ore mining, and building services.

Furthermore, when we compare the decline of unions internationally, it becomes clear that the rate, intensity, and timing of union decline do not correspond to the decline in manufacturing. In essence, the narrative that places globalization and automation as the primary drivers of union decline is overly simplistic and overlooks several other crucial factors.

The Workers' Perspective

Recent survey research affirms that workers' demand for unions remains high. Nearly half of nonunion workers have indicated that they would vote to have union representation if given the opportunity. This statistic highlights a significant mismatch between worker preferences and the realities of labor law. The labor law has failed to evolve in line with workers' interests and needs, resulting in a policy drift away from supporting union organizing and collective bargaining.

Policy Implications and Conclusions

Labor law's failure to adapt to changing external circumstances has resulted in a steady decline in its effectiveness in supporting workers' ability to pursue union organizing and collective bargaining. This trend has persisted despite majority support for reform in both houses of Congress and presidential support for reform.

The persistence of policy drift underscores the challenges workers face in exercising their rights to form and join unions. It reveals the complex interplay between labor law, corporate practices, and broader socioeconomic trends. As policymakers and stakeholders engage in discussions to address the erosion of workers' bargaining power, the analysis and insights provided in this chapter will be vital in informing the debate and guiding potential solutions. The task ahead lies in rectifying the shortcomings in current labor laws, ensuring they evolve to serve workers' interests and needs, and restoring the balance of power between employers and employees.

A: The erosion of private-sector unions in the United States is a complex issue influenced by various factors, including corporate practices and changes in labor law. While globalization and automation have often been cited as major drivers of union decline, empirical evidence suggests that these factors explain only a fraction of the decline. The erosion of unions extends beyond the manufacturing sector to non-manufacturing sectors and industries, indicating that other underlying causes are at play.

Corporate practices have played a significant role in the decline of private-sector unions. Employers have increasingly engaged in anti-union behavior, such as firing union activists and holding mandatory meetings to discourage unionization. They have also utilized the services of "union avoidance" consultants to impede organizing efforts. These practices, combined with legal changes that tilt labor law in favor of employers, have weakened the ability of workers to exercise their rights to form and join unions.

Legislative attempts to strengthen labor laws and address the decline of unions have been met with staunch opposition from the business community, resulting in legislative stalemate. The failure to enact meaningful reforms has hindered the effectiveness of the National Labor Relations Board (NLRB) and limited the accountability of employers for unfair labor practices.

International comparisons of union decline further support the notion that factors beyond globalization and automation have contributed to the erosion of unions. The decline in union coverage in non-manufacturing sectors and industries in various countries mirrors the trends observed in the United States.

Surveys indicate that there is significant demand for unions among nonunion workers, with nearly half expressing a desire for union representation. This highlights a disconnect between workers' preferences and the existing labor law framework, which has not evolved to adequately support workers' interests and needs.

Addressing the erosion of private-sector unions requires comprehensive policy solutions. Reforms should aim to rectify the shortcomings in labor laws, restore the balance of power between employers and employees, and ensure that workers have the freedom to exercise their right to form and join unions. These policy discussions should take into account the complex interplay between labor law, corporate practices, and broader socioeconomic trends to develop effective solutions that empower workers and strengthen their ability to advocate for their rights and interests.

In conclusion, understanding the erosion of private-sector unions and its impact on workers is crucial for developing policies that promote workers' rights and economic justice. By addressing the underlying causes, such as corporate practices and legal changes, policymakers and stakeholders can work towards creating a more equitable and supportive environment for unions to thrive, ultimately benefiting workers and fostering a fairer labor landscape.

4: The erosion of private-sector unions in the United States is a multifaceted issue with profound implications for economic inequality, wage stagnation, and worker rights. This phenomenon is attributed not just to the forces of globalization and automation but to a confluence of factors including corporate practices and legislative changes that have steadily shifted the balance of power towards employers.

Corporations have evolved strategies over the decades to resist unionization. Tactics such as firing union activists, holding mandatory meetings to dissuade union formation, and leveraging a burgeoning "union avoidance" industry have effectively thwarted unionization efforts. The legal landscape has enabled these practices, with labor laws that have progressively leaned towards employer interests and diluted worker rights. Even well-intentioned attempts to reform the law and strengthen unions have been stymied by a united front from the business community, resulting in a legislative stalemate that further impedes progress.

In addition to these domestic factors, an international comparison of union decline suggests that macroeconomic trends alone cannot explain the universal decline of unions. This international perspective underscores that the erosion of unions is not confined to the manufacturing sector or countries severely impacted by globalization. There's a pattern of decline in non-manufacturing sectors across various countries, indicating that the explanation for union decline transcends simplistic narratives around globalization and automation.

Importantly, the persistence of anti-union strategies and the skewed labor laws do not align with workers' attitudes towards unions. Surveys indicate a significant appetite for union representation among non-union workers, revealing a mismatch between the desires of the workforce and the realities of the labor law framework. This disconnect speaks to the policy drift in labor laws which have not evolved in step with worker preferences and societal needs.

Tackling this issue necessitates a multi-pronged approach. Policymakers need to address these systemic issues, rebalance the scales tipped heavily in favor of employers, and align labor laws more closely with the needs and desires of workers. This effort requires robust policy discussion that acknowledges the intricate interplay of labor laws, corporate practices, and societal trends to develop holistic solutions.

In essence, to mitigate the erosion of private-sector unions, efforts must be focused on creating labor laws that protect workers' rights, curbing corporate practices that hinder unionization, and encouraging societal recognition of the essential role unions play in ensuring worker rights and fostering economic equity. As we address these challenges, we lay the foundation for a more equitable labor landscape where the collective bargaining power of workers is restored, leading to fairer wages, improved working conditions, and reduced economic disparities.

Chapter 15

Outsourcing Jobs to Other Countries: Is Globalization a Threat to American Workers?

Introduction

W: The economic history of America tells a story of continuous labor shifts, starting from the post-Civil War era when New England's textile factories moved southwards, then, a century later, to countries like Mexico and Indonesia. Today, with globalization accelerating at an unprecedented pace, American jobs continue to relocate overseas to low-wage countries. The phenomenon of outsourcing, wherein American companies import goods they once produced domestically, has reshaped the U.S. economy and sparked debates about its implications on American workers.

Section One: The Historical Trajectory of Outsourcing

In the 1970s, American companies began outsourcing a range of factory work to other countries. Jobs in clothing, steel, toys, television sets, and computer hardware and chips migrated overseas. The trend accelerated in the 1990s with the implementation of free-trade agreements like NAFTA (North American Free Trade Agreement), which significantly reduced or eliminated tariffs, making foreign-made imports cheaper than American manufactured goods. The manufacturing sector now accounts for only 22 percent of all private enterprise output in the U.S., indicating a shift to a primarily service-based economy.

Section Two: The Digital Revolution and Outsourcing

The Internet revolution of the 1990s introduced a new dimension to outsourcing. The advent of high-speed telecommunications enabled a shift in many computer or knowledge-based services to overseas locations, marking what some have termed the "death of distance." The outsourcing trend gained further momentum during the boom of "dot-com" companies in the late 1990s. The first type of knowledge-based services to be outsourced was IT management, followed by customer service "call centers" and various "back office" operations such as data entry, accounting, and insurance claim processing.

Section Three: The New Frontiers of Outsourcing

In the current era, outsourcing is extending to high-tech and professional jobs, including software programming, paralegal work, financial investment research, X-ray and CAT-scan analysis, and drug testing. This shift is largely driven by cost-cutting needs to stay competitive. For instance, American software programmers' average annual income in 2004 was about $70,000, while their Indian counterparts earned approximately $8,000. India's English-speaking workforce, significant time-zone advantage, and substantial pool of college graduates have made it a leading destination for American outsourcing.

Section Four: The Impact and Future Implications

Despite the growing trend, the precise impact of outsourcing on American knowledge-based jobs remains uncertain due to a lack of comprehensive data. Available estimates suggest a relatively small but growing fraction of job losses due to outsourcing. Speculations range from 3.3 to 14 million knowledge-based jobs being at risk due to outsourcing between 2000 and 2015. This uncertainty calls for further research to understand the full scope of outsourcing's impact and formulate appropriate policy responses.

Conclusion:

As the U.S. economy continues its transformation, the question of whether outsourcing due to globalization poses a threat to American workers remains pertinent. Navigating the complexity of outsourcing requires a nuanced understanding of its historical progression, present circumstances, and potential future implications. The challenge lies in leveraging the benefits of a globalized economy while safeguarding American jobs and maintaining the nation's economic strength.

A: Outsourcing jobs to other countries and the broader issue of globalization remain significant topics of debate and analysis. While the information provided in the introduction and sections one to four covers key historical and contemporary aspects of outsourcing, there are additional perspectives and considerations to explore.

1. Global Supply Chains: Outsourcing is not limited to relocating jobs to low-wage countries. It is also intertwined with the concept of global supply chains, where different stages of production are distributed across multiple countries. Companies may choose to outsource specific tasks or components to take advantage of specialized skills or cost efficiencies. This fragmentation of production has become a dominant feature of global trade and offers benefits such as lower costs, increased efficiency, and access to new markets.

2. Technological Advancements: It is important to recognize that outsourcing is not solely a product of globalization but is also influenced by technological advancements. The digital revolution and advancements in communication technology have significantly facilitated outsourcing by enabling efficient collaboration across borders. Cloud computing, video conferencing, and remote work tools have made it easier to coordinate activities and manage global teams, making outsourcing a more viable option for many companies.

3. Job Creation and Innovation: While outsourcing has led to job losses in certain sectors, it is essential to consider the broader impact on employment. Globalization and outsourcing have also contributed to job creation, particularly in industries that benefit from lower costs or expanded market access. Additionally, outsourcing certain tasks can free up resources for companies to focus on higher-value activities, leading to innovation and the creation of new job opportunities.

4. Upgrading Workforce Skills: As jobs are outsourced, there is a need for American workers to adapt and acquire new skills that

are in higher demand. The shifting landscape of the labor market emphasizes the importance of investing in education, training, and retraining programs to equip workers with the skills needed for the evolving job market. Policies aimed at supporting workers in transitioning to new industries or acquiring advanced skills can mitigate the negative impact of outsourcing.

5. Policy Considerations: Effectively addressing the challenges posed by outsourcing requires a multifaceted approach. Policymakers need to strike a balance between promoting economic growth, protecting domestic industries, and ensuring job opportunities for American workers. This can involve a combination of measures such as implementing fair trade practices, investing in infrastructure and education, fostering innovation and entrepreneurship, and providing support for affected workers through social safety nets and reemployment programs.

In conclusion, while outsourcing has undoubtedly reshaped the U.S. economy and raised concerns about the impact on American workers, the phenomenon is multifaceted and interconnected with broader global trends. Understanding the complexities of outsourcing and its implications is crucial for formulating effective policies that promote economic growth, job creation, and workforce resilience in an increasingly interconnected world.

4:

1. The Polarization of Job Opportunities: The shifting labor market due to outsourcing can lead to the polarization of job opportunities. Jobs in the middle of the wage distribution, such as manufacturing and clerical jobs, are most likely to be outsourced, leading to an increased concentration of jobs at the high and low ends of the wage spectrum. This polarization can exacerbate income inequality and poses challenges for workers who lack the skills required for high-wage jobs.

2. Impact on Consumer Prices and Quality: While outsourcing can lead to job losses, it can also lower prices for consumers by reducing production costs. Additionally, companies might improve product quality or create new products by leveraging unique skills or technologies available in other countries. This aspect underscores the trade-offs inherent in outsourcing and globalization, where benefits often accrue to

consumers and businesses, while costs are borne more directly by displaced workers.

3. Role of Multinational Companies: Multinational corporations play a critical role in outsourcing. These companies can use their extensive resources and global networks to efficiently relocate jobs or production processes to countries where costs are lower. By doing so, they not only benefit from cost savings but also gain access to new markets, fostering further growth and profits. Understanding the motivations and strategies of these corporations can provide additional insights into the dynamics of outsourcing.

4. Climate Impact: The environmental implications of outsourcing are another dimension to consider. Longer supply chains may increase carbon emissions due to the transportation of goods across greater distances. Furthermore, lax environmental regulations in some countries can lead to more pollution as production shifts to these locations. Therefore, considering the environmental impact can add another layer to the analysis of outsourcing's benefits and drawbacks.

5. Inequality among Nations: While this article has primarily focused on the impact of outsourcing on American workers, it's also worth noting the effects on workers in other countries. Outsourcing can contribute to economic growth and poverty reduction in developing countries by creating job opportunities and attracting foreign investment. However, it can also perpetuate inequality between nations and lead to labor rights issues if workers in these countries are exploited due to weak labor laws and regulations.

Ultimately, outsourcing is a complex phenomenon embedded in the broader processes of globalization and technological change. To fully understand its impacts and implications, it's necessary to consider a broad range of perspectives and factors. It also calls for comprehensive and balanced policy solutions that address the various challenges and opportunities associated with outsourcing.

Chapter 16

Addressing the Challenges of Outsourcing: Strategies for a Balanced Economy

W: Outsourcing, often depicted as a double-edged sword, has stirred up a significant debate among economists, policymakers, and the public. On one side, it is hailed as a strategic tool that allows businesses to reduce costs and focus on their core competencies. On the other, it is seen as a menace causing job losses and wage depression, leading to public resentment and heightened economic uncertainty.

Lou Dobbs, a noted critic of outsourcing, argues that it is detrimental to the American middle class, threatening the country's economic strength by forcing U.S. workers to compete with low-wage workers in other countries. Conversely, several economists, including Greg Mankiw and Paul Krugman, contend that outsourcing could be a long-term boon to the economy, viewing it as an extension of international trade, which generally leads to economic growth and prosperity.

Economists who favor outsourcing argue that it only constitutes a small part of the economy. They emphasize that outsourcing is a two-way street – while the U.S. outsources services, other countries also outsource to the U.S., often more so. Lower prices resulting from outsourcing can benefit American consumers, stimulate competition, and spur innovation, leading to the creation of new high-paying jobs. Moreover, they point out that most job losses are not due to outsourcing but other economic factors.

However, the Economic Policy Institute, among others, caution against the potential pitfalls of outsourcing, notably the risk of the U.S. losing more service jobs than it gains and the challenge posed by countries like India, which is producing a greater number of engineers annually than the U.S.

Looking at these diverse perspectives, it becomes clear that a balanced, strategic approach is needed to navigate the complexities of outsourcing. Here are a few proposed strategies:

1. Promoting Research and Innovation: Federal investment in science, technology, and innovation is vital to ensure U.S. businesses continue to lead in creating high-tech, high-paying jobs. Providing tax credits to companies investing in research and

development can stimulate private sector innovation.

2. Reconsidering Trade Agreements: Critics of free-trade agreements argue for renegotiations to establish a "level playing field" with international labor and environmental standards. This would mitigate the issue of American businesses being undercut by low-wage, low-regulation economies.

3. Protectionism: While tariffs on imports can shield domestic industries from foreign competition, they could provoke retaliation, harming export-oriented sectors. Instead, removing tax breaks for companies that outsource work could be considered.

4. Enhanced Worker Support: As outsourcing is likely to continue, substantial investments in public education at all levels are crucial. Workers displaced due to outsourcing may need extended unemployment benefits and retraining to equip them for new jobs. Support mechanisms like unemployment insurance, health insurance, wage insurance, and retraining programs can soften the blow for those transitioning between jobs.

5. Safeguarding Security and Privacy: Legislations are required to protect the

security and privacy of personal information being handled abroad. This is particularly important in sectors like healthcare and finance where the sensitivity of data is high.

Outsourcing, like any economic phenomenon, presents both opportunities and challenges. By adopting a balanced approach, the U.S. can harness the benefits of globalization while mitigating its potential pitfalls, ultimately ensuring that the American economy continues to thrive in a rapidly evolving global landscape.

A: The strategies outlined above provide a starting point for addressing the challenges posed by outsourcing and achieving a balanced economy. However, it is important to consider additional factors and potential approaches to complement these strategies:

1. Foster Entrepreneurship and Small Business Growth: Supporting the growth of small businesses and entrepreneurship can diversify the economy and create new job opportunities. By providing access to capital, mentorship programs, and streamlined regulatory processes, policymakers can encourage innovation and promote the development of industries that are less susceptible to outsourcing.

2. Collaboration Between Government, Industry, and Academia: Close collaboration between these sectors can help identify emerging trends, skill requirements, and potential areas of growth. Partnerships can facilitate the development of industry-relevant education and training programs, ensuring that the workforce is equipped with the skills needed in the evolving job market.

3. Focus on High-Value-Added Services: While outsourcing has traditionally been associated with low-skilled manufacturing jobs, there is an opportunity to promote high-value-added services that are less easily outsourced. This includes fields like advanced research and development, design, engineering, creative industries, and specialized consulting services. Emphasizing these areas can create a competitive advantage for American workers and businesses.

4. Addressing Global Labor Standards: Encouraging international dialogue and cooperation on labor standards can help ensure fair competition and protect workers' rights globally. Engaging with other countries to promote fair wages, safe working conditions, and environmental

sustainability can level the playing field and reduce the incentive for outsourcing based solely on labor cost differentials.

5. Continuous Learning and Adaptability: Given the dynamic nature of the global economy, lifelong learning and adaptability are crucial for workers to remain competitive. Encouraging a culture of continuous learning, reskilling, and upskilling through accessible and affordable education and training programs can empower workers to adapt to changing job market demands and technological advancements.

6. Encouraging Domestic Consumption and Investment: Policies that promote domestic consumption and investment can strengthen the domestic market and create new job opportunities. This can include measures such as incentivizing businesses to invest in local communities, improving infrastructure to support economic growth, and fostering a culture of entrepreneurship and innovation.

It is important to recognize that addressing the challenges of outsourcing requires a comprehensive and multifaceted approach. No single strategy can fully resolve the complex issues involved. A combination of proactive policies, collaboration between stakeholders, and continuous adaptation to changing circumstances is essential to ensure a balanced economy that can navigate the impacts of outsourcing while fostering economic growth and protecting American workers.

4:

1. Future-Proofing the Economy: With rapid advancements in artificial intelligence and automation, the future landscape of work is expected to change dramatically. As a part of strategic planning, it's crucial to future-proof the economy by investing in sectors that are expected to grow and are resistant to outsourcing. This includes fields like renewable energy, advanced manufacturing, and healthcare. Simultaneously, education systems need to be aligned to prepare the workforce for these future jobs.

2. Investment in Infrastructure: A robust infrastructure can make the economy more competitive and reduce the incentives for outsourcing. Investing in areas such as transport, broadband connectivity, clean energy, and other foundational sectors can improve efficiency, stimulate economic activity, and create jobs.

3. Addressing Social and Regional Inequality: Outsourcing tends to affect certain

industries and regions more heavily than others. An effective strategy should address these disparities, ensuring that the benefits of economic growth are broadly shared. This can involve targeted support for hard-hit regions or industries, including economic diversification programs, localized retraining initiatives, and social support.

4. Role of Multinational Companies: Multinational corporations often play a key role in outsourcing. Policy measures may be necessary to ensure that these companies contribute fairly to the economy. This can involve measures such as corporate tax reform, incentivizing companies to retain or create jobs domestically, or promoting responsible business practices.

5. Strengthening Unions: Unions can play a crucial role in advocating for workers' rights, promoting fair wages, and providing a counterbalance to corporate power. Policies that strengthen the rights of workers to organize and negotiate collectively can help address some of the adverse impacts of outsourcing.

6. International Cooperation: Addressing the challenges of outsourcing is not just a domestic task; it also requires international

cooperation. Working with other countries through international organizations and forums can help establish global norms and standards that promote fair competition, protect workers' rights, and ensure sustainable development.

In conclusion, while outsourcing presents significant challenges, it also provides opportunities for the American economy to adapt and evolve. A strategic, comprehensive approach that draws on a variety of measures, coupled with continuous adaptation to changing circumstances, can help ensure a balanced economy that is resilient in the face of globalization and technological change.

Chapter 17

Artificial Intelligence: The Double-Edged Sword of Economic Progress

Introduction

W: The story of human progress has always been intertwined with technological innovation, and artificial intelligence (AI) represents the latest leap forward. The ripple effects of AI's rise are being felt across all sectors, acting as a catalyst for growth, innovation, and efficiency. However, like many transformative developments before it, AI is a double-edged sword. On one side, it has the potential to catapult us into an era of unprecedented prosperity; on the other, it raises significant concerns about job losses and growing wealth inequality.

Section One: AI and the Evolution of Job Markets

AI's capability to learn, predict, and automate has made it a powerful tool in an increasingly data-driven world. Sectors as diverse as healthcare, manufacturing, finance, and retail have all witnessed the effects of AI's integration, which has reshaped job roles and functions. While AI can create new opportunities and boost productivity, it's also poised to disrupt traditional job markets drastically. For instance, routine tasks, whether cognitive or manual, are most susceptible to automation, leading to the displacement of workers engaged in such roles. The varying impacts on different sectors and job types highlight the uneven ripple effects of AI across the job market.

Section Two: AI and Job Losses

History is replete with instances of technological advancements displacing jobs. From the industrial revolution to the advent of computers, each significant technological shift has initially displaced workers. However, the pace at which AI is advancing raises concerns about the adaptability of the job market and the workforce. Can new jobs be created at a rate that absorbs those displaced by AI automation? The answer is not straightforward and depends on many variables including the rate of AI development, adaptability of the workforce, and policy interventions.

Section Three: The AI Wealth Gap

Alongside job displacement, another concerning aspect of AI is its potential to exacerbate wealth inequality. The productivity gains and profits derived from AI primarily benefit capital owners, leading to a widening wealth gap. The rise of AI has also facilitated the emergence of 'superstar firms', whose market dominance and profit accumulation further intensify income inequality. If left unchecked, the AI-driven economic model could create an ever-widening chasm between the 'haves' and the 'have-nots.'

Section Four: Possible Solutions and Policy Interventions

Mitigating the downsides of AI requires a concerted effort from policymakers, educators, businesses, and society at large. Governments may need to play a regulatory role, ensuring the benefits of AI are broadly shared. This could involve taxation of AI gains to fund social safety nets, labor market policies to protect workers, and public investment in sectors less likely to be automated. On the education front, emphasis should be on lifelong learning, equipping individuals with skills needed for the jobs of the future. More radical propositions, such as the universal basic income, also warrant serious consideration.

Conclusion

The rise of AI presents a paradox — a powerful tool for growth and progress, yet a potential catalyst for job losses and wealth inequality. Striking a balance between these two extremes is the challenge of our era. The narrative of AI should not be one of dystopian despair, but of proactive adaptation. Through thoughtful policy, collective action, and foresight, we can aim to shape a future where AI serves as a tool for inclusive, sustainable progress rather than a harbinger of inequality.

A: The introduction and sections one to four provide a solid overview of the opportunities and challenges posed by artificial intelligence (AI). However, there are additional considerations and perspectives to be explored:

1. Skill Enhancement and Reskilling: As AI disrupts job markets, there is a need to focus on skill enhancement and reskilling programs to ensure the workforce remains adaptable and capable of leveraging AI technologies. Education systems and training initiatives should prioritize teaching skills that complement AI, such as critical thinking, creativity, complex problem-solving, and emotional intelligence. By nurturing these uniquely human skills, workers can collaborate effectively with AI systems and find new roles in the evolving job landscape.

2. Ethical and Responsible AI Development: As AI becomes increasingly pervasive, it is crucial to prioritize ethical considerations in its development and deployment. Measures

such as transparency, fairness, and accountability need to be integrated into AI systems to avoid biases, discrimination, and negative societal impacts. Standards and regulations can guide AI development to ensure that it aligns with ethical principles and serves the best interests of society.

3. Collaboration Between Humans and AI: Instead of perceiving AI as a complete replacement for human labor, there is an opportunity to explore collaboration between humans and AI systems. This collaborative model, known as "augmented intelligence," leverages the strengths of both humans and AI to achieve better outcomes. By working alongside AI, humans can focus on tasks that require creativity, empathy, and complex decision-making, while AI systems handle repetitive or data-intensive tasks.

4. Entrepreneurship and Innovation: AI presents opportunities for entrepreneurs and innovators to create new business models and industries. By harnessing the power of AI to solve complex problems and address societal needs, entrepreneurs can drive economic growth and job creation. Supportive policies, access to capital, and a nurturing ecosystem for startups can

facilitate the emergence of AI-driven entrepreneurial ventures.

5. Global Collaboration and Governance: AI is a global phenomenon that transcends national borders. International collaboration and governance frameworks are needed to address the global challenges associated with AI, including data privacy, cybersecurity, and the ethical use of AI in warfare. Multilateral efforts can help establish norms and guidelines that ensure responsible and accountable AI development worldwide.

6. Public Perception and Awareness: Promoting public understanding and awareness of AI is essential for fostering trust and acceptance. Effective communication about the capabilities, limitations, and potential impact of AI can help dispel misconceptions and address fears. This can involve educational campaigns, public discussions, and opportunities for public participation in AI policy and decision-making processes.

In conclusion, while AI brings immense potential for economic progress and innovation, it also poses challenges that need to be carefully navigated. A holistic approach, encompassing education, policy, ethics, and collaboration, is necessary to harness the benefits of AI while mitigating its negative impacts. By shaping AI development and adoption in a responsible and inclusive manner, society can strive towards a future where AI enhances human capabilities, fosters economic growth, and promotes equitable outcomes.

4:

1. Digital Inclusion: The transformative power of AI shouldn't widen the existing digital divide; rather, it should be harnessed to create a more inclusive digital economy. This requires strategies to ensure access to digital infrastructure, digital literacy, and digital services for all, including marginalized and vulnerable groups. By prioritizing digital inclusion, the benefits of AI can be shared more equitably.

2. Creating a Social Contract for AI: A social contract for AI can be an effective mechanism to outline the roles, responsibilities, and rights of different stakeholders, including AI developers, users, and those affected by AI technologies. This contract could address issues like who should bear the cost of retraining workers, how the economic benefits of AI should be

shared, and how to safeguard against AI misuse.

3. Promoting Transparency and Explainability in AI: The complex, opaque nature of some AI systems can make it difficult for users to understand how they work and make decisions. Promoting transparency and explainability in AI can build trust, ensure accountability, and enable people to challenge AI decisions that affect them.

4. Resilience to AI-Driven Cyber Threats: As the use of AI increases, so too does the potential for AI-driven cyber threats. This can include the use of AI to conduct sophisticated cyberattacks or the hacking of AI systems themselves. Strategies to build resilience to these threats can include developing secure AI technologies, enhancing cybersecurity skills, and fostering international cooperation on cybersecurity.

5. Environmental Impact of AI: AI technologies, particularly those that require large amounts of data and computing power, can have significant environmental impacts. Measures to mitigate these impacts can include promoting energy-efficient AI technologies, using renewable energy for AI

operations, and considering environmental factors in AI policy and decision-making.

6. AI and Democracy: The use of AI in the political sphere, for example in political campaigns or disinformation campaigns, can have implications for democracy. Policymakers and society need to navigate these challenges to ensure that AI supports rather than undermines democratic processes.

In conclusion, AI is more than just a technological or economic issue; it touches on all aspects of society, from the economy and education to ethics and democracy. Navigating the double-edged sword of AI requires an inclusive, multidimensional approach that brings together different perspectives and expertise. By doing so, we can aim to create a future where AI supports human flourishing, social progress, and economic prosperity.

Chapter 18

The Psychology of Billionaires: The Impact of Wealth on Mental Health

W: The psychology of billionaires—people who have amassed wealth beyond most people's comprehension—is complex and multi-faceted. While being extremely wealthy brings about many advantages, there are challenges tied to this level of affluence that are often overlooked.

What motivates billionaires and why do they continue to seek more wealth even when they have more than they could ever spend? A combination of factors including the drive for success, the desire for influence, and the fear of losing their status contribute to this relentless pursuit. This pursuit, however, can have significant impacts on their mental health, as well as on the wellbeing of their families.

Billionaires often exist in a high-pressure environment with a constant demand for success and achievement. This drive can lead to a phenomenon called the 'toxic money mindset', where an obsession to maintain and increase wealth dominates their thoughts and actions. They tend to prioritize making more money over having more time, despite studies showing that people who value time over money are generally happier and have healthier relationships.

This relentless pursuit of wealth can lead to decreased empathy, clouded moral judgment, and a constant state of comparison and competition. A sense of moral entitlement often characterizes these individuals, and they are likely to engage in unethical behaviors. This skewed focus on self-promotion and the lack of compassion towards others can contribute to a set of personality traits psychologists label as the 'dark triad': Machiavellianism, psychopathy, and narcissism.

The family dynamics in ultra-wealthy households can also contribute to mental health issues. Parents in such families are often absent due to work commitments or social obligations, leaving the upbringing of their children to nannies or boarding schools. Children from affluent families face unique pressures such as high expectations to excel, isolation from parents, and a lack of boundaries. They can easily access substances and alcohol, and are often preoccupied with material wealth and appearance. These circumstances can lead to higher rates of depression, anxiety, substance abuse, and other behavioral problems among affluent children.

A clear example of the potential negative impacts of affluence is the case of Ethan Couch, who was diagnosed with 'affluenza', a term that denotes irresponsibility caused by family wealth. Having grown up without facing repercussions for his behavior due to his family's wealth, Couch showed a deep sense of privilege and complete lack of responsibility.

While wealth can ensure access to the best healthcare, it doesn't guarantee health or happiness. The pressure and isolation associated with immense wealth often lead to suffering, pain, and mental health disorders. It's evident that behind the glamour and privileges associated with immense wealth, there lie unique and significant challenges.

A: The discussion on the psychology of billionaires and the impact of wealth on mental health sheds light on an often overlooked aspect of extreme affluence. Here are some additional insights to consider:

- The Hedonic Treadmill: The pursuit of wealth can become a never-ending cycle as individuals adapt to their newfound wealth and seek even greater levels of financial success to sustain their elevated lifestyle. This phenomenon, known as the hedonic treadmill, suggests that the initial euphoria of wealth wears off over time, leading billionaires to continually chase greater wealth as a means of maintaining their happiness and fulfillment.

- Social Isolation: While billionaires may be surrounded by luxury and social connections, they can still experience profound feelings of loneliness and isolation. The vast wealth gap between them and the general population can create barriers to forming genuine connections and lead to a sense of detachment from everyday experiences and struggles.

- Impact on Relationships: Wealth disparities within relationships, such as between billionaires and their partners, can introduce unique challenges. Power dynamics, differing priorities, and financial dependencies can strain relationships and contribute to feelings of resentment and disconnection. It is not uncommon for wealthy individuals to face difficulties in establishing and maintaining authentic relationships built on trust and mutual understanding.

- Philanthropy and Purpose: Some billionaires seek to find meaning and purpose through philanthropy and giving back to society. Engaging in philanthropic endeavors can provide a sense of fulfillment and contribute to improved mental well-being by focusing on making a positive impact on the world. However, it is crucial for billionaires to strike a balance between philanthropy and personal well-being, ensuring they address their own mental health needs alongside their charitable efforts.

- Cultivating Self-Awareness and Emotional Intelligence: Developing self-awareness and emotional intelligence can help billionaires navigate the psychological challenges associated with extreme wealth. Being conscious of one's own emotions, motivations, and values can contribute to more fulfilling relationships, a greater sense of purpose, and a more balanced approach to wealth accumulation and its impact on well-being.

- Shifting Perspectives on Success and Fulfillment: Society's definition of success is often closely tied to financial wealth, leading individuals to prioritize material accumulation as a measure of achievement. Encouraging a broader definition of success that encompasses personal well-being, meaningful relationships, and contributions to society can help individuals, including billionaires, find a more balanced and fulfilling approach to their lives.

Understanding the complex interplay between wealth, mental health, and personal fulfillment is crucial for individuals, families, and society at large. By acknowledging the challenges and promoting open conversations around wealth and well-being, we can foster a more empathetic and supportive environment that encourages a holistic approach to success and mental health for billionaires and the wider population.

4:

- Societal Perception and Judgment: With their lives often under public scrutiny, billionaires face the pressure of constant societal judgment and expectations. While public opinion varies, billionaires often encounter criticism for their wealth, lifestyle choices, and their actions (or lack thereof) in tackling social issues. This public pressure can intensify feelings of stress, anxiety, and isolation, further impacting their mental health.

- Wealth Stigma and Denial of Struggles: There's a common belief that wealth should directly equate to happiness, leading many to dismiss or undermine the mental health struggles of the ultra-wealthy. The stigma around "rich people problems" can make it challenging for billionaires to seek help or express their emotional distress, as they fear their issues will not be taken seriously or will be dismissed due to their privileged financial status.

- Mental Health Services and Confidentiality: While billionaires have the resources to afford the best healthcare services, the issue of confidentiality can be a significant concern when seeking mental health support. Fear of information leakage can deter them from accessing professional help, further exacerbating their mental health issues. Tailored mental health services that guarantee privacy can be critical for this group.

- The Role of Therapy and Counseling: For billionaires, therapy and counseling can offer a safe space to express their fears, insecurities, and anxieties. Therapists who specialize in counseling for high-net-worth individuals understand the unique challenges that come with immense wealth and can provide targeted strategies to manage stress, relationship dynamics, and self-perception issues.

- The Importance of Financial Literacy and Education: For billionaires, particularly those who have inherited their wealth or achieved it at a young age, understanding how to manage their wealth responsibly and sustainably is essential. Education around wealth management, including the psychological aspects of wealth, can help them navigate the potential pitfalls and pressures that come with being ultra-rich.

In summary, while significant wealth can open doors to numerous opportunities and privileges, it's not an immunity against mental health issues. On the contrary, the unique pressures and challenges tied to immense wealth can exacerbate mental health problems. It's essential for society to foster an understanding and empathetic outlook towards these challenges and for mental health professionals to develop appropriate support mechanisms. Acknowledging that mental health issues affect individuals across the wealth spectrum is a step towards promoting comprehensive mental health support and understanding.

Chapter 19

Luck or Skill - The Role of Unfair Advantages

The debate on whether success is a product of luck or hard work is as old as the concept of success itself. While it's impossible to discount the significance of either, a broader perspective highlights the value of both, and the importance of leveraging one's unique strengths or "unfair advantages".

Drawing upon the success stories of billionaires like Elon Musk, Warren Buffett, Bill Gates, and Oprah Winfrey, we observe a complex interplay between innate skills, work ethic, and circumstances that seem purely chance-driven. While critics often claim these success stories owe much to luck, the reality is far more nuanced.

Take Elon Musk, for example. Born to an affluent family, he is criticized by some as having merely reaped the benefits of his birth. However, a deeper look into his life reveals a troubled childhood and a tireless drive to innovate and disrupt industries. Luck may have had a hand in his life, but it didn't create PayPal, SpaceX, Tesla, or Neuralink; those were products of his vision, talent, and relentless determination.

Warren Buffett, often revered as the Oracle of Omaha, attributes a significant portion of his success to luck, including the timing and location of his birth, and his natural inclination toward capital allocation. Yet, none of these factors negate his hard work and meticulous investment strategies. Similarly, Bill Gates's access to a computer in the late '60s and his connections with IBM can't undermine his innovation and pioneering role in the tech industry.

Oprah Winfrey, who hails from a significantly less privileged background, used her natural talent for speaking and storytelling to build a media empire, transforming her life dramatically. Her "luck" was in realizing her inherent skills early on and having the perseverance to utilize them optimally.

These stories underline the importance of what authors Ash Ali and Hasan Kubba call "unfair advantages". These advantages can be classified under the MILES Framework, representing Money, Intelligence & Insight, Location & Luck, Education & Expertise, and Status. These elements can provide a unique edge, aiding individuals to leverage their circumstances and strengths to their advantage.

The debate on luck vs. skill shifts significantly when viewed through the lens of "unfair advantages".

Recognizing and harnessing these advantages can be instrumental in attaining success, making it clear that it's not merely about being lucky or working hard, but rather about understanding and leveraging one's unique position and capabilities in the pursuit of their goals.

A: The discussion on the role of luck and skill in success, as well as the concept of "unfair advantages," opens up interesting perspectives on the complexity of achievement. Here are some additional points to consider:

1. Overcoming Adversity: While individuals may have certain advantages, they often face significant challenges and obstacles along their journey. Overcoming adversity requires resilience, determination, and the ability to adapt. Even with "unfair advantages," individuals must demonstrate the drive and work ethic necessary to capitalize on those advantages and turn them into tangible success.

2. Social and Cultural Factors: Success is not solely determined by individual characteristics or advantages. Social and cultural factors play a significant role in shaping opportunities and outcomes. Factors such as race, gender, socioeconomic background, and access to resources can

significantly impact an individual's trajectory. Recognizing these systemic influences is essential for understanding the broader context in which success and advantages are realized.

3. Collaboration and Networks: Success often relies on connections and collaborations. Building and leveraging social networks can create opportunities and amplify one's abilities. The support and mentorship of others can play a crucial role in unlocking potential and expanding opportunities, particularly for individuals who may face systemic barriers.

4. Long-Term Perspective: The debate between luck and skill can be reframed by considering the long-term impact of decisions and actions. While luck may play a role in short-term outcomes, sustained success is often the result of consistent effort, continuous learning, and strategic decision-making. Luck alone is unlikely to sustain success over the long term, highlighting the importance of skill development and personal growth.

5. Ethical Considerations: The concept of "unfair advantages" raises ethical questions about the responsibility that comes with privilege. Those who possess significant

advantages have an opportunity and, some argue, an obligation to use their position to create positive change and promote greater equity. Ethical decision-making involves recognizing the impact of one's advantages and actively seeking ways to contribute to a more just and inclusive society.

6. Intersectionality: It is important to acknowledge that advantages and disadvantages intersect and interact with one another. Individuals may possess certain advantages in one area of life while facing disadvantages in others. Recognizing the complexity of intersecting advantages and disadvantages helps to challenge simplistic narratives about success and the role of luck and skill.

In conclusion, the interplay between luck, skill, and "unfair advantages" in achieving success is multifaceted and context-dependent. While acknowledging the role of advantages in success, it is crucial to consider the broader systemic factors and ethical dimensions at play. By recognizing the complexity of success and promoting fairness and inclusivity, individuals and society can work towards a more equitable and supportive environment where everyone has the opportunity to thrive.

4: Exploring the dynamics of luck, skill, and unfair advantages in the context of success reveals the intricate nature of these elements. Further insights might consider the following:

- Luck as a Product of Action: There's a saying, "The harder I work, the luckier I get." This phrase, often attributed to Thomas Jefferson, underscores the potential for hard work to generate opportunities that may be perceived as luck. Engaging with the world, creating networks, pursuing learning, and taking risks often lead to unexpected positive outcomes. Thus, while luck may be a factor in success, it is often intertwined with action and effort.

- Skill Acquisition and Deliberate Practice: Successful individuals often dedicate immense time and effort to honing their skills. Renowned psychologist Anders Ericsson coined the term "deliberate practice" to describe the focused, systematic training methods used by experts to achieve mastery in their fields. This type of dedicated effort is a counterpoint to the notion that success is primarily the result of luck or inherent talent.

- Role of Growth Mindset: The concept of a "growth mindset," introduced by psychologist Carol Dweck, suggests that abilities can be developed through dedication and hard work. This view fosters a love for learning, resilience, and a willingness to embrace challenges — all of which are critical for long-term success. It further implies that recognizing and leveraging one's unfair advantages doesn't mean resting on one's laurels. Instead, it involves actively cultivating one's potential.

- The Problem with Survivorship Bias: When discussing success, it's essential to be mindful of survivorship bias, the logical error of concentrating on the people or things that made it past some selection process while overlooking those that did not. By focusing solely on the success stories, we might falsely assume that luck or a specific set of advantages are the primary drivers of success, while discounting the many examples where similar factors did not result in the same outcome.

- Broadening the Definition of Success: Success is often narrowly defined as wealth, fame, or power. However, there are many other forms of success that are equally valuable but often overlooked, such as contributions to community, personal growth, strong relationships, mental health, or contentment. Redefining success can also change the calculus of luck and unfair advantages.

In summary, while unfair advantages can provide a head start, the journey to success is often paved with hard work, resilience, deliberate practice, and a growth mindset. Moreover, it's important to understand that luck, skill, and unfair advantages can have different impacts depending on the individual and context. Recognizing this complexity can lead to a more nuanced understanding of success and the multiple paths leading to it.

Chapter 20

Divisions and Disparities: How Race and Culture are Exploited to Disempower the Working Class

W: As we traverse an era marked by growing economic disparity, a consistent narrative has emerged — one that illustrates the insidious exploitation of racial and cultural differences to further segregate the working class. This calculated ploy operates as an engine for the relentless accumulation of wealth by a privileged minority, consequently marginalizing the majority.

The underpinnings of this societal division lie in the long-standing and systematic manipulation of racial and cultural distinctions, cleverly leveraged to instigate discord within the working class. This is a calculated divide-and-conquer strategy aimed at veiling the commonality of economic struggles endured by the working class, which transcend racial and cultural divides. By kindling cultural fears and racial tensions, attention is masterfully diverted from the expanding chasm of wealth inequality and the systemic economic structures that safeguard it.

Historically, the exploitation of racial and cultural differences has been a potent tool to impede the unification of the working class. From the oppressive era of the Jim Crow laws in the South designed to marginalize Black workers, to the vilification of immigrant labor throughout the 19th and 20th centuries, these orchestrated divisions have invariably enabled the ruling class to fortify their stronghold on wealth and power.

Several contemporary case studies further underscore how this manipulation continues unabated. Consider the controversy surrounding immigration. By casting immigrants as threats to economic stability, attention is cunningly shifted away from corporate practices that depress wages and breed job insecurity. Similarly, the contentious debate around affirmative action often inflames fears of 'reverse discrimination' among white workers, conveniently obscuring the overarching issue of income inequality that indiscriminately affects all races.

The media serves as a critical instrument in propagating this divisive narrative. Sensationalized headlines and polarized debates often serve to accentuate racial and cultural differences, driving a wedge between various factions within the working class. This media-induced division fortifies the narrative that the economic challenges are the outcomes of 'the other', effectively diverting focus from the underlying systemic issues.

Recognition of the manipulative exploitation of race and culture to divide the working class is a crucial step towards dismantling the structures that allow wealth accumulation to remain concentrated. A unified front among working-class individuals across racial and cultural lines is essential to effectively address the systemic economic disparities impacting everyone. By redirecting attention from these divisive tactics to common economic goals, the working class can initiate a powerful challenge to the structures that perpetuate wealth inequality.

The route to transformative change demands a collective effort. Only by acknowledging and actively resisting these divisive narratives, can we move towards economic and social systems that are truly fair and equitable, regardless of race or culture. It is through unity, not division, that we can hope to disrupt the economic structures that perpetuate these disparities.

A: The exploitation of racial and cultural differences to disempower the working class is a deeply troubling phenomenon that has persisted throughout history and continues to shape our society today. By deliberately fueling divisions and prejudices, those in positions of power manipulate the working class, diverting attention away from the underlying economic disparities that affect individuals across racial and cultural lines.

Historically, racial segregation and discriminatory laws, such as the Jim Crow laws, were employed to marginalize Black workers and maintain a system of economic inequality. Similarly, the vilification of immigrant labor has been used as a means to undermine the unity of the working class and protect the interests of the privileged few. These examples demonstrate how the exploitation of racial and cultural differences has served as a powerful tool to perpetuate wealth and power imbalances.

Contemporary issues like the debate on immigration and affirmative action highlight the ongoing manipulation of racial and cultural divisions. By framing immigrants as economic threats or stoking fears of reverse discrimination, attention is diverted from the larger structural issues of income inequality and economic exploitation that affect individuals of all races. Media sensationalism and polarized debates further exacerbate these divisions, reinforcing the false narrative that economic challenges are the result of differences between racial and cultural groups.

Recognizing and challenging these manipulative tactics is crucial for creating a more equitable society. Unity among the working class, transcending racial and cultural lines, is essential for addressing systemic economic disparities and dismantling the structures that perpetuate wealth inequality. By rejecting divisive narratives and focusing on common economic goals, individuals can come together to challenge and transform the systems that breed inequality and exploitation.

It is imperative to understand that the fight against economic disparities cannot be won without confronting the racial and cultural divisions that have been exploited for centuries. Building bridges of solidarity and empathy across diverse communities is a powerful way to dismantle the barriers that perpetuate inequality. By embracing a collective effort for change and actively resisting divisive narratives, we can strive towards a society that upholds fairness, justice, and equal opportunity for all, regardless of race or culture.

4: The exploitation of racial and cultural differences to disempower and divide the working class is not only a historical reality but a pressing contemporary issue. It demonstrates how societal divisions can be manipulated to maintain a status quo that favors a wealthy minority, diverting attention from the pressing issue of economic inequality.

Historically, race has been used as a tool to segregate and control the working class. This is evident in the institution of the Jim Crow laws, which marginalized Black workers, to the vilification of immigrants as threats to economic stability. These divisions are not naturally occurring, but rather, have been strategically orchestrated to maintain power structures. The ruling classes have long understood that a united working class is a potent threat to the status quo.

In the present day, we continue to see this manipulation of racial and cultural differences. The controversy surrounding immigration, for instance, is often framed in a way that presents immigrants as economic threats. The debate over affirmative action likewise stokes fears among certain groups, exacerbating divisions and obscuring the broader issue of wealth disparity.

The media plays a significant role in reinforcing and perpetuating these divisive narratives. By sensationalizing cultural and racial differences and fueling polarizing debates, the media can create a sense of division within the working class. This aids in maintaining the narrative that economic challenges are due to the perceived threat of 'the other', rather than systemic issues within our economic structures.

However, recognizing these divisive tactics is a critical step towards challenging the system that perpetuates wealth inequality. This demands unity among the working class, across racial and cultural lines, to confront systemic economic disparities. It requires shifting focus from the divisive narratives and towards common economic objectives. By doing so, the working class can challenge the structures of power that perpetuate wealth inequality.

This path towards change is not easy and requires collective effort and solidarity. It involves acknowledging and resisting these divisive narratives and striving towards economic and social systems that are fair and equitable for all, regardless of race or culture. This unity is the antidote to the divisions and disparities fueled by the exploitation of racial and cultural differences. By coming together as one, the working class can disrupt the structures that maintain these economic disparities and work towards a more equitable society.

Chapter 21

Greed and the Philosophy of Wealth

W: Greed, as an excessive or rapacious desire for wealth, presents a moral dilemma. A balance between the pursuit of wealth and the basic virtues of charity, kindness, and solidarity with others is necessary for ethical living. As Hesiod, the Greek poet, suggests, the principle of moderation applies to every aspect of life, including wealth and property.

The ownership of property is generally accepted as a right. The ability to possess things — such as a phone, a car, or clothing — is generally recognized as a basic economic freedom. However, when the accumulation of wealth begins to create extreme disparities, causing societal tension between the super-rich and the impoverished, it is necessary to question when the desire for wealth transforms into greed.

17th-century English philosopher John Locke proposed a "fair usage" view of property. His philosophy can be distilled into three criteria:

1. The property must be capable of being used before it spoils.
2. The acquisition of property must leave "good and enough" for others.
3. The property must result from one's own labor and effort.

This perspective, though seemingly straightforward, does not account for the complexities of modern economic systems. With the advent of digital banking, money neither spoils nor becomes scarce. This disrupts Locke's traditional view of property and wealth and potentially justifies rampant accumulation of wealth. Locke's philosophy then arguably underpins the philosophy of greed.

The notion of greed being an inherent aspect of humanity is ancient, tracing back to the times of Plato and finding modern representation in theories of evolutionary psychology. However, philosopher Peter Singer presents a counter-argument. He acknowledges the role of competitiveness in evolution but suggests that cooperation and productive relationships are equally vital. Singer proposes that a healthy desire to do good, work hard, and succeed becomes greed when the quest for material wealth overshadows all other aspects of life. It manifests when one's life is dominated by the constant need for more—more wealth, more possessions—at the expense of personal relationships and compassion.

The challenge lies in recognizing and acknowledging the presence of greed in one's life. While it's easy to lose perspective in our day-to-day lives, maintaining an awareness of the broader societal context is essential. As Singer highlights, even individuals considered poor in the West often live better than royalty did for centuries. Being mindful of the world's inequality and reflecting on one's own consumption and accumulation habits are key steps in resisting the insidious slide into greed.

Greed transforms into an issue of morality when it replaces our common sense of compassion and solidarity. It's when the pursuit of property and wealth becomes more important than basic human virtues—when the accumulation of more wealth and the attainment of material possessions matter more than the welfare of others. This recognition and subsequent self-reflection can serve as powerful tools to combat greed and work towards a more balanced approach to wealth and property.

A: The discussion on greed and the philosophy of wealth provides valuable insights into the moral dimensions of wealth accumulation. Here are additional perspectives to consider:

1. Ethical Responsibilities of the Wealthy: With great wealth comes great responsibility. Wealthy individuals have the capacity to make significant contributions to society, alleviate suffering, and address systemic issues. Embracing a philosophy of philanthropy and social impact can help redirect the pursuit of wealth towards positive change. By actively engaging in charitable endeavors, investing in social causes, and advocating for equitable economic systems, billionaires can use their resources to promote social well-being and reduce the negative impacts of wealth inequality.

2. Redefining Success and Happiness: The pursuit of wealth and material possessions as a primary source of happiness is often misguided. Research in positive psychology highlights the importance of intrinsic values such as personal growth, meaningful relationships, and a sense of purpose in fostering long-term well-being. By shifting the focus from external markers of success to internal fulfillment and social connection, individuals can find greater satisfaction and reduce the allure of excessive wealth accumulation.

3. Systemic Change: Addressing greed and wealth inequality requires systemic changes in economic and political structures. This includes implementing policies that promote fair taxation, reduce wealth disparities, and ensure access to essential services for all members of society. Additionally, reforming corporate governance, increasing transparency, and holding businesses accountable for their social and environmental impact can help foster a more equitable distribution of wealth.

4. Cultivating Empathy and Compassion: Overcoming greed requires a shift in mindset towards greater empathy and compassion. Developing an understanding of the challenges faced by those less fortunate and actively engaging in acts of kindness and support can help individuals connect with their broader human community. Empathy can be nurtured through education, exposure to diverse perspectives, and fostering a sense of global citizenship.

5. Promoting Ethical Business Practices: Business leaders play a crucial role in shaping the ethical landscape of wealth accumulation. By prioritizing ethical business practices, treating employees fairly,

and embracing sustainable models, business leaders can demonstrate that success can be achieved without compromising ethical principles. Creating a corporate culture that values social responsibility and ethical conduct can contribute to a more equitable and compassionate economic system.

6. Educating Future Generations: Incorporating lessons on ethical decision-making, responsible consumption, and the social impact of wealth in educational curricula can help instill values of fairness and compassion in future generations. By raising awareness and nurturing a sense of social responsibility from an early age, societies can work towards reducing the allure of excessive wealth and fostering a more equitable distribution of resources.

In conclusion, addressing greed and the moral implications of wealth requires a multifaceted approach that encompasses personal reflection, systemic changes, and a collective commitment to social well-being. By redefining success, promoting ethical behavior, and fostering empathy, individuals and society as a whole can strive towards a more balanced and compassionate approach to wealth and property.

4: A critical perspective to consider in this conversation is the sociocultural paradigm that often glorifies the accumulation of wealth, sometimes to the point of excess. From media portrayals of the wealthy lifestyles to the cultural obsession with the "American Dream" of financial success, society frequently promotes the notion that wealth is directly correlated with happiness, prestige, and value.

The mainstream narrative often overlooks the moral implications of excessive wealth accumulation and underplays the societal cost of economic inequality. This cultural lens can fuel the perception that greed is not only acceptable but even desirable, as it is associated with personal success and achievement. Reversing this narrative requires promoting values of empathy, equity, and social responsibility in public discourse and the media.

The ethical implications of wealth accumulation also intersect with issues of social justice and equity. The wealth disparities observed globally are not just a reflection of individual actions but also systemic inequities ingrained in societal structures. Economic systems and policies often favor the rich, perpetuating wealth accumulation at the top and exacerbating income inequality.

In light of this, the conversation around greed and the philosophy of wealth should not be confined to individual attitudes and behaviors. Instead, it needs to extend to systemic and structural reforms aimed at promoting a more equitable distribution of resources. Policies such as progressive taxation, inheritance taxes, and wealth redistribution measures can help level the playing field and mitigate the consequences of extreme wealth accumulation.

Simultaneously, the role of billionaires in society must also be critically examined. The philanthropic endeavors of the ultra-wealthy, while often well-intentioned, can inadvertently create power imbalances and perpetuate the idea that societal problems can be solved through charity alone. Instead, a more sustainable approach is to advocate for fair economic systems that address the root causes of inequality.

Ultimately, a balanced and ethical approach to wealth accumulation involves not only personal introspection and responsibility but also a collective commitment to creating a fairer society. This includes advocating for equitable economic systems, promoting a culture of empathy and solidarity, and valuing contributions to society beyond monetary wealth.

It is also important to recognize that money in itself is not inherently evil; instead, it is the extreme desire for wealth, the relentless pursuit of more at the expense of others, that becomes morally problematic. By promoting a more balanced, compassionate, and ethical approach to wealth, society can foster a healthier relationship with money that benefits not just individuals, but the broader community as well.

Chapter 22

The Philosophical Critique of Greed: From Antiquity to the Present

W: The philosophers of antiquity were renowned for their contemplations on ethics and virtue, and many were deeply critical of greed and the unrestrained pursuit of wealth. Greed, in its essence, is the insatiable desire for wealth and material possessions, often leading to a disregard for fairness, equality, and other moral principles. A vast array of philosophical teachings - spanning from the ancient Greek philosophers to modern moral and political theorists - has served to warn humanity against this corrosive impulse.

The enigmatic figure of Socrates, immortalized through the writings of his student Plato, consistently questioned the societal norms and the prevalent overemphasis on material wealth. He advocated a life of virtue and morality, insisting that the constant thirst for more wealth would invariably lead to spiritual bankruptcy.

Plato himself was a fervent critic of greed. In his seminal work "The Republic", Plato challenged the unjust behaviors prevalent among the affluent, underlining the potential harm of unchecked desires. He envisaged a just society where such detrimental impulses were curtailed for the collective benefit.

Following in the intellectual footsteps of his teacher, Aristotle too was wary of excessive material desire. His doctrine of the "golden mean" in "Nicomachean Ethics" emphasized the importance of moderation. Virtue, for Aristotle, was a mean between two extremes - both excessive and deficient wealth were equally problematic and potentially conducive to moral decay.

Epicurus, often misunderstood as a proponent of hedonism, actually cautioned against the uncontrolled pursuit of wealth. He believed that simple pleasures, tranquility, and friendships were the cornerstones of a contented life, whereas excessive desires, like greed, could only engender pain and anxiety.

The teachings of Stoicism, propagated by Stoic philosophers like Seneca, Epictetus, and Marcus Aurelius, emphasized the cultivation of self-control as a tool for overcoming destructive emotions such as greed. They upheld virtue over material wealth and advocated living in harmony with nature.

Buddhist philosophy, as put forth by scholars like Nagarjuna and Vasubandhu, identified "tanha" or "trishna" (the thirst or desire) as a cause of suffering, encompassing the concept of greed. They advocated the practice of "dana" (giving) as an antidote to this.

Moving into the modern era, Karl Marx critiqued capitalism for the inherent exploitation often driven by greed. His vision was of a society where wealth is distributed according to need, not greed.

In his seminal work "A Theory of Justice," John Rawls articulated a critique of the unequal distribution of wealth. His philosophy promotes policies that benefit the least advantaged in society, subtly arguing against the greed leading to stark wealth disparities.

In conclusion, from the stoas of ancient Athens to contemporary lecture halls, philosophers have persistently cautioned against greed. The relentless pursuit of wealth and material possessions, they warned, often leads to a disregard for essential moral principles and the collective good. In the context of the billionaires' increasing wealth and influence, such philosophical insights become especially poignant, calling for a careful re-evaluation of our societal norms and personal priorities.

A: Throughout history, philosophers have offered profound critiques of greed and the relentless pursuit of wealth. Their teachings provide timeless wisdom and serve as reminders of the moral and ethical implications of unchecked material desires.

These philosophers understood that greed, with its insatiable appetite for wealth and possessions, could lead individuals astray from virtuous and meaningful lives. Socrates, Plato, and Aristotle all emphasized the importance of moderation, balance, and the cultivation of virtues as antidotes to the corrosive nature of greed. They recognized that excessive wealth and the uncontrolled pursuit of material possessions could erode moral character and undermine the well-being of individuals and society.

Stoic philosophers, such as Seneca and Epictetus, advocated for the practice of self-control and the cultivation of inner tranquility as a means to overcome destructive emotions like greed. They encouraged individuals to find contentment and fulfillment through virtuous actions and alignment with nature, rather than the accumulation of material wealth.

In Eastern philosophies, such as Buddhism, the concept of greed is seen as a fundamental cause of suffering. Scholars like Nagarjuna and Vasubandhu highlighted the importance of practicing generosity and cultivating detachment from material possessions as a means to transcend the destructive nature of greed.

Modern philosophers like Karl Marx and John Rawls extended the critique of greed to the socio-political realm. Marx exposed the exploitative nature of capitalism, highlighting how greed and the pursuit of profit often result in the oppression of the working class. Rawls argued for a more just society that prioritizes the well-being of the least advantaged, challenging the prevailing narrative of greed-driven inequalities.

The philosophical critique of greed invites us to reflect on our values and reconsider the role of material wealth in our lives. It prompts us to question the prevailing emphasis on accumulation and to consider alternative measures of success and fulfillment. These insights are particularly relevant in the context of billionaire influence, where the concentration of wealth and the pursuit of self-interest can undermine the principles of fairness, equality, and collective well-being.

By drawing on the wisdom of these philosophers, we can engage in a thoughtful examination of our societal norms, personal aspirations, and the ways in which we contribute to the betterment of our communities. Their teachings remind us that true fulfillment and a just society are not found in the relentless pursuit of material wealth, but in the cultivation of virtues, empathy, and a genuine concern for the well-being of all.

4: The discourse on greed, materialism, and wealth has been deeply embedded in philosophical thought from antiquity to the present, traversing across various cultures and socio-political contexts. Philosophers from Socrates to John Rawls have provided critiques of unchecked desire and the relentless pursuit of wealth, offering timeless insights into the ethical implications of these tendencies.

The figure of Socrates, whose thoughts have been immortalized by his student Plato, offered a critique of the societal norms of his time, particularly the overemphasis on material wealth. He proposed a life of virtue and morality over wealth accumulation, an idea that was advanced by Plato in his writings, notably in "The Republic". The wisdom of these philosophers reverberates in our current society, warning against the spiritual void that can be created by an unrestrained pursuit of wealth.

Aristotle's doctrine of the "golden mean" has stood the test of time as a practical guide to living a balanced life. He postulated that both excessive and deficient wealth could lead to moral decay, arguing for a middle path that fosters moral health and well-being. Epicurus, too, cautioned against the blind pursuit of wealth, advocating instead for a life of simple pleasures and tranquility.

The stoic philosophers, who emphasized self-control and virtue, also provide a rich tapestry of wisdom. They advocated for living in harmony with nature, drawing attention to the perils of destructive emotions like greed. In parallel, Eastern philosophies like Buddhism identify desire or "tanha" as a root cause of suffering, offering practices such as "dana" (giving) as an antidote.

The philosophical discourse of greed extends into the modern era with Marx's critique of capitalism and the exploitation it engenders due to unchecked greed. Rawls, too, highlights the inequitable distribution of wealth and the socio-political consequences that arise from it. His philosophy urges for societal structures that benefit the least advantaged, subtly critiquing the greed that exacerbates wealth disparities.

Thus, from ancient Athens to contemporary society, philosophers have consistently offered a robust critique of greed. In the light of the expanding wealth and influence of billionaires, these philosophical insights warrant a closer look. They call for a re-evaluation of societal norms and personal priorities, highlighting the need to balance the pursuit of wealth with moral and ethical considerations.

These philosophical teachings can serve as guides in navigating our materialistic world, calling for introspection and ethical considerations in our pursuits. Their wisdom illuminates the path to a more equitable society, encouraging the cultivation of virtues over the accumulation of wealth. They remind us that the unchecked pursuit of wealth often leads to societal disharmony and personal discontentment, urging instead for a balance between material wealth and moral integrity. In our era of billionaire influence, these teachings can serve as a critical reminder of the importance of wealth distribution, fairness, and collective well-being.

Chapter 23

Religious Teachings and Warnings Against Greed

W: Regardless of the diversity of cultural contexts and historical eras, virtually all major world religions carry teachings that warn against the pitfalls of greed and excessive wealth. These ancient wisdom traditions present a stark contrast to our contemporary, often materialistic society, highlighting the timeless tension between worldly desires and spiritual ideals.

Christianity, for example, is abundant with teachings warning against avarice. The Bible, in Matthew 6:24, sternly warns, "No one can serve two masters. Either you will hate the one and love the other, or you will be devoted to the one and despise the other. You cannot serve both God and money."

Similarly, Islam cautions against the relentless pursuit of material wealth. In Surah Al-Hakumut-Takathur (102:1-2) of the Quran, it is stated: "Competition in [worldly] increase diverts you until you visit the graveyards."

The Jewish tradition also holds a warning for those driven by greed. The Tanakh, in Proverbs 28:25, proclaims, "A greedy man stirs up strife, but the one who trusts in the Lord will be enriched."

Hinduism, with its diverse set of teachings, also recognizes the danger of greed. The Bhagavad Gita 16.21 warns, "There are three gates leading to this hell – lust, anger, and greed. Every sane man should give these up, for they lead to the degradation of the soul."

In Buddhism, greed is highlighted as a source of suffering in the Four Noble Truths. Greed (lobha) is categorized as one of the "Three Poisons" that cause suffering and hamper the path towards enlightenment.

Sikhism echoes similar sentiments. The Guru Granth Sahib, the central text of Sikhism, admonishes, "The world is deceived by the love of wealth and possessions, and so it passes its life in vain."

Other Eastern philosophies such as Taoism and Confucianism also counsel against wealth and greed. The Tao Te Ching states, "He who is contented is rich." Similarly, Confucian teachings found in the Analects propose, "The determined scholar and the man of virtue will not seek to live at the expense of injuring their virtue. They will even sacrifice their lives to preserve their virtue complete."

Zoroastrianism, one of the world's oldest religions, suggests renunciation of the material world as a path towards righteousness as stated in the Avesta. Jainism, known for its strict ascetic practices, promotes non-attachment to material possessions as a way of life.

The Baha'i faith too, discourages materialistic pursuits. In the writings of Baha'u'llah, it is written, "O SON OF BEING! If thine heart be set upon this eternal, imperishable dominion, and this ancient, everlasting life, forsake this mortal and fleeting sovereignty."

Even in Shinto, a religion deeply connected with nature and harmony, excessive wealth and greed contradict its core teachings of harmony, respect, and purity.

These religious teachings serve as moral compasses, warning their followers about the spiritual dangers of excessive wealth and greed. They remind us that unchecked accumulation of wealth often leads to moral corruption, social inequality, and spiritual bankruptcy. They advocate for contentment, balance, and generosity, ideals that stand in stark contrast to the modern narratives often associated with billionaire influence and power.

A: Religious teachings from various traditions offer valuable insights into the dangers of greed and the pursuit of excessive wealth. Across major world religions, there is a consistent theme of caution against placing material possessions and wealth above spiritual values and the well-being of others.

These teachings serve as timeless reminders that the relentless pursuit of wealth can lead to moral corruption and spiritual degradation. They call for individuals to prioritize values such as contentment, generosity, and humility, which stand in opposition to the insatiable desire for accumulation.

By emphasizing the transient nature of material wealth and its potential to divert individuals from more meaningful pursuits, religious teachings invite reflection on the true sources of fulfillment and happiness. They remind us that wealth and possessions, while important for meeting our basic needs and responsibilities, should not become the sole focus of our lives.

Moreover, these teachings shed light on the societal implications of unchecked greed and wealth concentration. They warn against the harm caused by inequality, social divisions, and the erosion of compassion that often accompany the unbridled pursuit of wealth. By highlighting the destructive consequences of greed, religious teachings promote a more equitable and harmonious society.

In the context of billionaire influence, these religious teachings offer a critical perspective. They remind us that the accumulation of vast wealth comes with responsibilities and ethical considerations. The influence wielded by billionaires in shaping policies and governance raises questions about fairness, justice, and the well-being of society as a whole. Religious teachings caution against the abuse of power and the exploitation of others for personal gain.

By reflecting on these teachings, individuals and societies can strive for a more balanced approach to wealth and influence. This entails finding a harmonious integration of material and spiritual values, pursuing economic prosperity while remaining mindful of the ethical implications and social impact of our actions.

In an era marked by growing wealth disparities and the concentration of power in the hands of a few, the wisdom contained within religious teachings offers guidance and encourages a reevaluation of societal priorities. It calls for a collective commitment to address inequality, promote social justice, and foster a more compassionate and equitable world.

4: In this chapter, the author explores the teachings from various religious and philosophical traditions that warn against the dangers of greed and the relentless pursuit of wealth. These warnings, present across different cultures and eras, offer a stark contrast to the contemporary, often materialistic, society, bringing forth a discussion on the tension between worldly desires and spiritual ideals.

Christianity, Islam, Judaism, Hinduism, Buddhism, Sikhism, Taoism, Confucianism, Zoroastrianism, Jainism, and the Baha'i faith – each offers unique perspectives on the perils of excessive wealth accumulation and greed. They advocate for values such as contentment, humility, generosity, and the spiritual enrichment of the self over material enrichment. The teachings across these religions emphasize that the unchecked pursuit of wealth often leads to moral, social, and spiritual corruption.

Considering the current context of growing wealth disparities, these religious teachings provide a critical lens to evaluate the societal implications of concentrated wealth. The undue influence billionaires can exert in policy-making and governance, often driven by their economic interests, echoes the spiritual warnings against excessive wealth accumulation. The narratives often associated with billionaire influence and power, in many ways, contradict the ancient wisdom of contentment and generosity that these religious teachings advocate.

Religious teachings, which often serve as moral and ethical compasses, call for a balance between material desires and spiritual well-being. They offer insights on the transient nature of worldly possessions and caution against allowing material wealth to become the center of our lives. While wealth in itself isn't inherently problematic, the teachings suggest that its unchecked pursuit could divert individuals from their moral and ethical responsibilities.

Moreover, these teachings resonate with the modern-day societal challenges of wealth inequality and socio-economic disparities. They warn of the moral corrosion, social divisions, and erosion of compassion that often follow the unbridled pursuit of wealth. They serve as reminders that extreme wealth accumulation, without considerations of fairness, justice, and overall societal well-being, can lead to significant societal discord.

In the era of billionaire influence, these teachings could guide us to reassess our societal values and priorities. They push us towards pursuing economic prosperity while remaining grounded in ethical values and social responsibility. They remind us that while wealth can bring power and influence, it also brings with it a responsibility to ensure that such influence is used in a manner that is fair, just, and beneficial for society as a whole.

Therefore, religious teachings can offer a foundation for constructing a more equitable society. They underscore the need for both individuals and societies to consciously balance material desires with spiritual fulfillment and to strive for economic prosperity without losing sight of ethical obligations and social impact. In a world marked by wealth disparities, these teachings could guide us towards a more compassionate, fair, and inclusive society.

Chapter 24

Is it Moral to be a Billionaire?

Introduction

W: The concept of billionaire status evokes a range of emotions and opinions. While some view billionaires as symbols of success, innovation, and economic growth, others question the morality of accumulating such vast wealth in a world marked by inequality and social challenges. This chapter aims to examine both perspectives and delve into the pros and cons of being a billionaire from an ethical standpoint.

Pros of Billionaire Status

1. Economic Growth and Job Creation: One of the primary arguments in favor of billionaires is their potential to drive economic growth and job creation. Through their entrepreneurial endeavors and investments, billionaires can generate wealth, innovate industries, and create employment opportunities. They often fund startups, launch new businesses, and support research and development, leading

to technological advancements and economic expansion.

2. Philanthropy and Charitable Contributions: Billionaires possess the financial resources to make significant philanthropic contributions and support charitable causes. Many billionaires engage in philanthropy, establishing foundations and organizations that address societal issues such as poverty, education, healthcare, and environmental sustainability. Their donations can have a transformative impact, helping to uplift communities and improve the lives of disadvantaged individuals.

3. Innovation and Entrepreneurship: Billionaires often embody the spirit of innovation and entrepreneurship. Their vision, risk-taking abilities, and resource allocation contribute to the creation of groundbreaking products, services, and technologies. They invest in research and development, drive competition, and fuel economic progress. The successes of billionaires can inspire and motivate others to pursue entrepreneurial endeavors, fostering a culture of innovation.

4. Economic Influence and Investment: Billionaires wield considerable economic

influence, which can shape markets and industries. Their investments can provide capital to fund startups, support struggling companies, and drive economic growth. By allocating their wealth strategically, billionaires can have a positive impact on industries, spur innovation, and contribute to overall economic stability.

5. Job Compensation and Incentives: Billionaires often lead large corporations and employ thousands of individuals. They are responsible for setting compensation structures and providing incentives for their employees. Through competitive salaries, bonuses, and stock options, billionaires can attract and retain top talent, fostering a motivated and skilled workforce.

Conclusion

The pros of billionaire status revolve around the potential for economic growth, job creation, philanthropy, innovation, and economic influence. While these arguments highlight certain positive aspects, it is essential to balance them with a critical examination of the ethical implications and potential drawbacks associated with extreme wealth accumulation. The following sections will explore the cons and delve deeper into the moral considerations surrounding billionaire status.

Cons of Billionaire Status

1. Camping Analogy: Hoarding of Resources

An analogy often used to illustrate the cons of billionaire status is that of a camping trip. Imagine a group of individuals embarking on a camping adventure, where everyone is expected to contribute their fair share of provisions. However, one person in the group accumulates an excessive amount of food, water, and supplies, leaving the rest of the campers with limited resources. This scenario raises ethical concerns about the fairness and equity of wealth distribution. Critics argue that billionaires, akin to the camper hoarding provisions, concentrate a disproportionate amount of resources, leaving many others with limited access to basic necessities and opportunities for socioeconomic advancement.

2. The Question of "When is Enough Enough?"

Another critical consideration when discussing the morality of billionaire status is the concept of sufficiency. At what point does one's wealth become excessive, surpassing the bounds of personal security and well-being? Critics argue that accumulating billions of dollars when one could live comfortably with a fraction of that wealth reflects an excessive pursuit of wealth for its own sake. In a world grappling with poverty, inequality, and unmet social needs, the question arises as to whether billionaires have a moral responsibility to redistribute their wealth and address systemic societal challenges.

3. Reflection on Previous Chapters

Throughout this book, we have explored various perspectives on wealth, income inequality, taxation, and the role of billionaires in society. Previous chapters have shed light on how economic systems and policies tend to favor the wealthy, exacerbating income disparities and hindering social mobility for the less privileged. We have also examined religious teachings, philosophical arguments, and historical data that caution against excessive greed, advocate for fairer wealth distribution, and highlight the negative consequences of extreme wealth concentration.

By synthesizing the insights from earlier chapters, it becomes evident that the moral implications of billionaire status extend beyond individual acts of philanthropy. The systematic inequalities perpetuated by wealth disparities, the negative impacts on social cohesion, and the potential for undue political influence raise concerns about the morality of accumulating such vast fortunes.

Conclusion

While billionaires may contribute to economic growth, innovation, and philanthropy, the cons of billionaire status cannot be ignored. Analogies like the camping trip highlight the ethical dilemma of one individual hoarding resources, raising questions about fairness and equity. Moreover, the concept of sufficiency prompts us to consider when wealth accumulation becomes excessive and whether billionaires have a moral obligation to address societal challenges. When reviewing the insights gathered from previous chapters, it becomes increasingly clear that the current state of extreme wealth concentration and income inequality raises significant moral concerns.

A: The discussion on the morality of being a billionaire encompasses a wide range of perspectives and considerations. It is important to recognize that the arguments presented in favor of billionaire status, such as economic growth, philanthropy, innovation, and job creation, highlight certain positive aspects of extreme wealth accumulation. However, it is equally important to critically examine the ethical implications and potential drawbacks associated with such vast fortunes.

The analogy of the camping trip illustrates the concerns about wealth concentration and the unfair distribution of resources. Critics argue that billionaires, by accumulating a disproportionate amount of wealth, contribute to income inequality and limit opportunities for socioeconomic advancement for others. This raises questions about the fairness and equity of wealth distribution in a society where basic necessities and opportunities for growth should be accessible to all.

Another consideration is the concept of sufficiency and the question of when wealth becomes excessive. Critics argue that accumulating billions of dollars when a fraction of that wealth would suffice for personal security and well-being reflects an excessive pursuit of wealth for its own sake. This prompts reflection on the moral responsibility of billionaires to address systemic societal challenges and redistribute their wealth for the benefit of society as a whole.

By reflecting on previous chapters exploring wealth, income inequality, taxation, and the role of billionaires in society, a broader perspective emerges. The systematic inequalities perpetuated by extreme wealth concentration, the negative impacts on social cohesion, and the potential for undue political influence raise significant moral concerns. It is important to consider the larger societal implications and the need for fairer wealth distribution to address the systemic challenges faced by many.

In conclusion, while recognizing the potential benefits associated with billionaire status, it is crucial to weigh them against the ethical considerations and drawbacks. The camping analogy, the concept of sufficiency, and the insights gathered from previous chapters shed light on the moral implications of extreme wealth accumulation and income inequality. Ultimately, a comprehensive examination of the morality of being a billionaire requires a nuanced understanding of the societal impact and the responsibility of those with vast fortunes to contribute to the collective well-being.

4: The discourse on the morality of billionaire status is a multidimensional one, spanning economics, sociology, and ethics. Here are some additional points to consider:

Pros of Billionaire Status

1. Billionaires as Role Models: It's important to acknowledge the cultural narrative that often positions billionaires as aspirational figures, embodying the "American Dream" or similar concepts of financial success and upward mobility. These narratives emphasize hard work, innovation, and resilience, which can inspire others to strive for success. However, these narratives often overlook systemic inequalities that may prevent many from achieving similar levels of success.

2. Potential for Large-scale Impact: The philanthropic potential of billionaires is vast, with the capacity to tackle significant global issues at scale, in a manner that is difficult for most individuals or even governments to accomplish.

However, this leads to questions about the potential for billionaires to exert undue influence over societal priorities and public policy.

Cons of Billionaire Status

1. The Role of Luck and Privilege: Critics argue that becoming a billionaire often involves a significant amount of luck or privilege, including access to education, social networks, and capital, among other advantages. This perspective challenges the narrative of billionaires as entirely self-made and raises ethical questions about wealth accumulation in the face of systemic inequality.

2. Undue Influence: The accumulation of extreme wealth can lead to undue political influence, allowing billionaires to shape policies that may further their interests at the expense of wider society. This undermines democratic principles and reinforces existing inequalities.

3. Wealth Inequality and Social Cohesion: Extreme wealth concentration can contribute to social unrest, as vast disparities in wealth are often perceived as unfair. This can erode social cohesion and trust within a society.

Reflecting on the ethics of being a billionaire also requires an examination of the societal structures that allow for such vast wealth accumulation. If being a billionaire is deemed immoral due to the associated wealth inequality and social impact, then this raises questions about the economic and political systems that enable this level of wealth concentration in the first place.

In conclusion, the question of whether it's moral to be a billionaire extends beyond individual billionaires to encompass systemic issues of wealth distribution, social inequality, and the influence of money on democratic processes. These factors need to be considered when assessing the morality of billionaire status, highlighting the importance of broader societal reform in addressing these ethical concerns.

Flaws in the United States Political System

W: I believe it's critically important to initiate a conversation about the inherent issues within the US political system, particularly as they contribute to the widening wealth gap. Several structural flaws in our political system have a direct impact on wealth inequality.

For example, lobbying and campaign financing often lead to laws and regulations that disproportionately favor the wealthy. Moreover, the limited representation of socioeconomically diverse communities in political offices can result in policies that don't adequately address the financial struggles of the average American citizen.

Addressing these political structures and their implications is a necessary step towards effectively managing the wealth disparity issue. By working to reform our political system, we can strive for a more equitable distribution of wealth and opportunities in our society. This conversation, while complex and challenging, is essential to creating a more equitable future for all.

Chapter 25

The Flaws in a Two-Party Political System - Multifaceted Issues Trapped in Binary Options

W: The two-party political system is deeply ingrained in countries like the United States. This binary setup places people into broad categories of "us" versus "them", often oversimplifying the complexities of human perspectives and societal issues. However, the challenges and intricacies of modern governance increasingly reveal cracks in this model.

To begin, the binary structure of a two-party system limits nuanced discussion. Political issues are multifaceted and diverse, yet a two-party system reduces them to simple for-or-against stances. This can cause significant challenges when dealing with complex problems such as healthcare reform, immigration policy, and climate change. These matters demand a spectrum of options and consideration, rather than a mere dichotomy of positions.

The two-party system also fosters an adversarial culture that can undermine collaborative efforts.

The inherent "us versus them" mentality can lead to polarization, where compromise is seen as betrayal rather than a path to consensus. Rather than fostering constructive debate and problem-solving, this system often devolves into partisan bickering and gridlock.

Moreover, it may limit representation. Not all political beliefs can be adequately captured by two monolithic parties. A citizen may agree with one party on fiscal policy, but align more with the other party on social issues. This forces individuals to prioritize some beliefs over others when voting, potentially leading to dissatisfaction and disengagement.

Finally, the two-party system can discourage third parties and independent voices. These parties struggle to gain traction in a system that tends to marginalize those outside the binary framework. This limits political diversity and could stifle innovative ideas that could emerge from outside the two major parties.

In light of these challenges, it's crucial to explore alternative models and reforms that could accommodate the complexity of modern political issues and diverse viewpoints. This might involve implementing ranked-choice voting, encouraging coalition governments, or changing the way electoral districts are drawn. Such changes may help to disrupt the "us versus them" narrative and cultivate a political climate that genuinely values nuanced discussion and collaboration.

A: The discussion on the flaws of a two-party political system provides insights into the limitations and challenges inherent in such a model. Here are some additional points to consider:

1. Diverse Representation: A two-party system may not adequately represent the diversity of a nation's population. It can overlook the voices and perspectives of minority groups, resulting in the underrepresentation of certain communities. A more inclusive political system should strive to ensure that all citizens have a fair chance to be heard and that their concerns are taken into account in decision-making processes.

2. Stagnation and Resistance to Change: The two-party system can create a sense of stability, but it may also foster resistance to change. Major policy shifts or reforms can be difficult to achieve when they challenge entrenched positions held by the two dominant parties. This can lead to a lack of adaptability and hinder progress on pressing issues that require innovative solutions.

3. Limited Policy Options: A binary political system often narrows the range of policy options available for consideration. It may exclude alternative perspectives or innovative ideas that could contribute to more effective governance. Opening up the political landscape to include a broader spectrum of parties and perspectives can foster a more robust and dynamic policy debate.

4. Voter Apathy and Disillusionment: The polarized nature of a two-party system can lead to voter apathy and disillusionment. When voters perceive that their choices are limited to two imperfect options, they may become disengaged from the political process. This can undermine democracy by reducing participation and weakening the connection between citizens and their elected representatives.

5. Long-Term Impact: A two-party system can perpetuate a cycle of alternating power between two dominant parties, making it challenging for new parties or independent candidates to gain significant influence. This lack of rotation in power may lead to a sense of complacency or entitlement within the established parties, potentially

hindering the fresh perspectives and ideas needed for effective governance.

6. Global Perspective: It's worth noting that the two-party system is not universal and that many democracies around the world have adopted different models. Some countries employ multi-party systems, proportional representation, or hybrid systems to accommodate diverse political viewpoints and foster greater representation and collaboration.

In conclusion, while the two-party system has long been a staple of certain political landscapes, it is crucial to critically assess its limitations and explore alternative models that can better address the complexities of modern governance. By fostering inclusivity, encouraging a broader range of policy options, and cultivating a culture of collaboration, political systems can better serve their citizens and enhance the democratic process.

4: The analysis of the two-party system raises thoughtful considerations regarding its flaws. Here are further points to ponder:

1. Compromise and Moderation: In theory, a two-party system can push parties towards the middle of the political spectrum to appeal to the majority of voters. However, in practice, this isn't

always the case. Polarization can often push parties further apart, leaving a gap in the center where moderate voices struggle to be heard.

2. Power Dynamics: The concentration of power within two major parties can lead to an imbalance in the political landscape. This power dynamic can influence policy direction and decision-making processes, potentially marginalizing the voices of smaller interest groups or those advocating for change.

3. Accountability and Transparency: While the "us versus them" dynamic of a two-party system can foster adversarial politics, it also creates clear lines of accountability. With only two primary parties to consider, it can be easier for voters to attribute responsibility for political actions. However, the lack of alternatives might also lead to lower accountability, as voters might feel that they have no other viable option.

4. Role of Media: The media plays a significant role in shaping the narrative in a two-party system. The binary nature of the system can perpetuate a polarized media environment, potentially

exacerbating divisions and contributing to the "echo chamber" effect, where individuals are exposed mainly to viewpoints that align with their own.

5. Electoral Reforms: While the text touched upon some reforms, others include the concept of a mixed-member proportional system, which combines elements of proportional representation and first-past-the-post voting. Such a system could potentially provide greater representation for smaller parties while maintaining the benefits of single-member districts.

6. Political Education: Greater emphasis on political education can help voters understand the complexities of political issues and the importance of their vote, promoting informed decision-making and possibly increasing engagement with the political process.

In summary, while a two-party system has its challenges, it also presents opportunities for reform and evolution. By examining these issues critically and with an open mind, society can strive for a more representative and equitable political system. Understanding these complexities can help in formulating strategies to address the flaws while building upon the strengths of the system.

Chapter 26

Gerrymandering and Its Threat to Democracy

W: Gerrymandering, a term coined in the 19th century, remains one of the most persistent threats to fair representation in democratic systems today. It's a practice where political boundaries are manipulated to favor one party or class, thereby distorting the electoral process and undermining the democratic principle of equal representation.

In the United States, the redrawing of electoral district boundaries, also known as redistricting, happens every decade following the census. Ideally, this is done to ensure that districts remain representative of their populations. It helps to maintain equal populations across districts, comply with laws such as the Voting Rights Act, and reflect the changing demographics of a state's population. However, this process can be hijacked and used as a tool for gerrymandering, creating maps that heavily favor one political group over another.

Gerrymandering can take several forms, but the two most common tactics are 'cracking' and 'packing'. Cracking involves spreading voters of a particular type among many districts in order to dilute their voting power, while packing involves concentrating like-minded voters in one district to reduce their influence in other districts. Despite what may seem unusual shapes of districts, it's essential to understand that not all oddly-shaped districts are gerrymandered, and even regularly shaped districts can be skewed heavily in favor of one party.

In the past decade, gerrymandering has notably influenced the balance of power in Congress and many state legislatures. For example, despite Democrats winning the majority of the statewide congressional vote in Pennsylvania, the congressional map guaranteed Republicans a significant number of seats. Similar situations arose in Michigan, North Carolina, and Wisconsin. While gerrymandering can favor either Republicans or Democrats, depending on who controls the redistricting process, it ultimately deprives the public of fair representation.

Particularly concerning is the impact of gerrymandering on communities of color. The prevalence of residential segregation and racially polarized voting patterns mean that these communities can be specifically targeted to gain partisan advantages. Furthermore, the Supreme Court's 2019 decision in Rucho v. Common Cause, which effectively barred challenges to partisan gerrymandering in federal court, opened the door for discrimination under the guise of partisan strategy.

Unfortunately, the problem is expected to worsen as technology advances. Modern algorithms and voter data allow map drawers to manipulate redistricting with surgical precision. The lack of legal framework adjustments to reflect changing demographics further exacerbates the issue, as new multiracial voting coalitions in diverse suburbs become vulnerable targets.

To combat gerrymandering, comprehensive reform is needed. Bills like the Freedom to Vote Act, which aims to enhance transparency, protect communities of color, and ban partisan gerrymandering in congressional redistricting, represent steps toward curtailing the negative impacts of gerrymandering. Urgent action is needed to ensure that democratic representation remains fair and unbiased.

A: Gerrymandering is a pressing issue that threatens the integrity of democratic representation. Here are some additional insights and perspectives to consider:

1. Impact on Voter Confidence: Gerrymandering erodes public trust in the electoral process. When voters perceive that the boundaries of their districts have been deliberately manipulated to favor one political party, they may become

disillusioned and disengaged from politics. This undermines the fundamental principles of democracy and can lead to a sense of apathy and frustration among citizens.

2. Partisan Polarization and Gridlock: Gerrymandering contributes to partisan polarization and gridlock in legislatures. By creating safe districts that heavily favor one party, it reduces the incentive for elected officials to appeal to a broader range of voters and seek compromise. This can lead to more extreme positions and hinder the ability to pass meaningful legislation that addresses the needs and concerns of the entire population.

3. Suppression of Minority Voices: Gerrymandering can disproportionately impact minority communities, particularly communities of color. By diluting their voting power or packing them into a limited number of districts, their ability to elect representatives who can effectively advocate for their interests is undermined. This perpetuates systemic inequalities and can suppress the voices of historically marginalized communities.

4. Technological Advancements and Redistricting: As technology continues to advance, the potential for more sophisticated and precise gerrymandering techniques increases. Access to detailed voter data and powerful mapping algorithms allows map drawers to manipulate boundaries with unprecedented precision. This highlights the urgency of implementing robust legal frameworks and safeguards to prevent abuse and ensure fair representation.

5. Role of Judicial Oversight: The role of the judiciary in addressing gerrymandering is crucial. However, the issue of partisan gerrymandering has proven challenging for courts to navigate. Determining the line between acceptable political considerations in redistricting and unconstitutional partisan manipulation is complex. Clear and consistent legal standards are needed to guide the judicial evaluation of gerrymandering claims.

6. Grassroots Movements and Public Awareness: Grassroots movements and advocacy groups have played a vital role in raising awareness about gerrymandering and pushing for reform. By mobilizing public support and

advocating for fair and transparent redistricting processes, these efforts contribute to creating a more inclusive and representative democracy.

In conclusion, addressing gerrymandering requires comprehensive reform, including legislation that promotes transparency, protects the rights of minority communities, and establishes clear standards for redistricting. By prioritizing the principles of fairness, representation, and equal voice, democratic systems can ensure that the power of voters is respected and that the electoral process remains a true reflection of the will of the people.

4: Delving deeper into the issue of gerrymandering, here are a few more points to contemplate:

1. Political Power and Incumbency: Gerrymandering can entrench political power and reinforce incumbency. By drawing district lines that favor a particular party or candidate, the odds of the incumbent party remaining in power increase. This could potentially lead to complacency and a lack of competition, undermining the democratic principle that power should be contestable.

2. Influence on Policy and Spending: Politicians elected from gerrymandered districts, where they enjoy a safe seat, may have less

incentive to be responsive to their constituents' needs. This could lead to imbalanced policy decisions and public spending that favor certain groups over others, further exacerbating social inequalities.

3. Negative Effect on Bipartisanship: Gerrymandering often results in "safe" districts for one party or another, resulting in elected officials who are less motivated to compromise or engage in bipartisan cooperation. This could contribute to the kind of political polarization and legislative gridlock that hampers the effective functioning of democratic institutions.

4. Need for Independent Commissions: The introduction of independent redistricting commissions can be a step toward limiting gerrymandering. These non-partisan bodies can be tasked with drawing electoral district boundaries, reducing the risk of manipulation by self-interested politicians. Several states have already implemented such commissions with varying degrees of success.

5. Public Awareness and Activism: Enhancing public awareness about the issue of gerrymandering is critical. Civil society

organizations, media outlets, and educational institutions have key roles to play in shedding light on this practice and fostering greater civic engagement. Grassroots activism can also play a significant part in pushing for reforms at the local, state, and national levels.

6. International Comparison: It's worth noting that gerrymandering isn't a problem exclusive to the United States. Other democracies also grapple with similar challenges, though the specifics may differ based on their electoral systems. Comparative analysis can provide useful insights into different strategies for mitigating the impact of gerrymandering.

In conclusion, gerrymandering is a complex issue that poses significant challenges to the democratic principle of equal representation. However, through legal reforms, technological safeguards, public awareness, and political will, it is possible to curtail its negative impacts and ensure a fairer democratic process.

Chapter 27

Disproportionate Representation and the 60-Senate-Vote Threshold - Flaws in the U.S. Political System

W: One of the principal foundations of the United States political system is the idea of equal representation; however, this principle doesn't always translate perfectly in practice. Particularly in the Senate, issues arise from the body's design that can result in unequal representation and challenging legislative processes.

Unequal Representation

Firstly, the U.S. Senate gives equal representation to each state, regardless of its population. This means that California, with a population of approximately 39.5 million, gets the same number of senators as Wyoming, which has around 580,000 inhabitants. Consequently, this system overrepresents less populated states, allowing the senators of these states to wield a disproportionately large amount of influence.

For instance, a senator from Wyoming represents far fewer people than a senator from California, meaning that each Wyomingite's vote is more powerful in the Senate than a Californian's vote. This structure diverges from the principle of "one person, one vote," a cornerstone of democratic fairness, and tends to skew policymaking towards the interests of less populated states.

The 60-Senators Threshold

Another facet of the Senate that draws criticism is the 60-vote threshold to invoke cloture and end a filibuster. Filibustering is a parliamentary procedure unique to the U.S. Senate, where senators can speak for unlimited time to delay or prevent a vote on a proposal. It's a tool often used by the minority party to block legislation they strongly oppose.

To overcome a filibuster, 60 of the 100 senators must vote for cloture. This requirement often presents a substantial barrier to the passage of legislation, even when there is a clear majority in favor. The 60-vote rule makes it harder to pass bills and can lead to legislative gridlock, especially in times of deep partisan polarization.

These elements of the Senate's structure, while essential aspects of the U.S. political system, have drawn criticism for their potential to undermine the principle of equal representation and the efficiency of legislative processes. They represent key challenges to be grappled with in the ongoing evolution of U.S. democracy.

A: The issues of disproportionate representation and the 60-senate-vote threshold in the U.S. political system raise important concerns about the fairness and functionality of the system. Here are some additional perspectives to consider:

1. Implications of Unequal Representation: The unequal representation in the Senate can lead to disparities in policy outcomes. Smaller states with fewer population sizes often have different priorities and concerns than larger states. This can result in policy decisions that do not necessarily align with the preferences and needs of the majority of the population. It raises questions about the democratic principle of majority rule and the equitable distribution of political power.

2. Changing Demographics and Representation: The disparities in representation become more pronounced as demographic shifts occur. Population growth and migration patterns can lead to significant imbalances in the number of constituents represented by each senator. This raises questions about the ability of the Senate to effectively address the evolving needs and interests of a diverse and changing society.

3. Filibuster and Legislative Gridlock: The 60-senate-vote threshold required to invoke cloture and overcome a filibuster has the potential to obstruct the legislative process. While the filibuster can serve as a tool to protect minority rights and promote deliberation, its excessive use can lead to legislative gridlock and hinder the ability of the majority to enact their policy agenda. This can frustrate public expectations for action on pressing issues and contribute to public disillusionment with the political process.

4. Democratic Representation vs. Minority Rights: The tension between democratic representation and protecting minority rights is at the core of these issues. While the Senate's structure ensures that smaller states have a voice, it can also lead to an imbalance where a minority of the population holds disproportionate power. Balancing the need for equitable representation with the protection of minority rights is a complex challenge that requires careful consideration.

5. Potential Reforms: There have been ongoing discussions about potential reforms to address these flaws in the U.S. political system. Some proposals include revisiting the apportionment of Senate seats based on

population size, modifying the filibuster rule, or exploring alternative voting mechanisms. These reforms aim to strike a better balance between equal representation and effective governance.

6. Public Engagement and Reform: Recognizing these flaws in the political system, it is crucial for citizens to remain engaged and advocate for meaningful reforms. Public pressure, grassroots movements, and a broader national conversation about the future of democratic representation can drive discussions and encourage policymakers to explore potential changes that promote fairness, accountability, and effective governance.

n conclusion, addressing the issues of disproportionate representation and the 60-senate-vote threshold requires thoughtful deliberation and potential reforms that strike a balance between democratic representation, protecting minority rights, and facilitating efficient decision-making. By critically examining the flaws of the political system, there is an opportunity to foster a more equitable and functional democracy that better serves the interests and aspirations of the American people.

4: The concerns around disproportionate representation and the 60-Senate-vote threshold in the U.S. political system present multi-faceted debates. Here are some additional points to consider:

1. Role of the Senate: It's important to remember the historical and constitutional reasons behind the equal representation of states in the Senate. The Founding Fathers designed the Senate to ensure that each state, regardless of size, had an equal voice in the federal legislative process. This was intended to balance the more population-sensitive representation in the House of Representatives. The challenge is how to reconcile this design with the principle of "one person, one vote" in a way that maintains the balance of powers while also ensuring democratic fairness.

2. Impacts on Partisanship: Disproportionate representation can exacerbate partisanship. Senators from smaller, more homogenous states may feel less pressure to moderate their positions and appeal to a broader base, which can contribute to political polarization. The influence of less populous states, which often lean heavily towards one party, could further entrench partisan divides in the Senate.

3. Influence of Minority Rule: The 60-vote threshold to end a filibuster essentially allows for minority rule. This can not only stall legislation but also has the potential to undermine public faith in democratic processes if a minority of senators can block legislation supported by a majority of the public.

4. The Importance of Compromise: The filibuster, despite its potential for misuse, does carry an implicit call for consensus-building and compromise. By requiring a supermajority for cloture, the Senate encourages cross-party dialogue and can prevent unilateral decision-making. The key is to balance this need for compromise with the necessity of efficient governance.

5. Long-term Repercussions: The effects of both unequal representation and the 60-vote threshold are not just limited to the Senate. They can have ripple effects on the judiciary, as Senate approval is required for federal judge and Supreme Court appointments. This can lead to an imbalance in the judiciary, further affecting the fairness and representation of the overall U.S. political system.

6. International Perspective: Looking beyond the U.S., many democracies around the world face similar dilemmas in trying to balance representation, minority rights, and effective governance. Each has different mechanisms in place to address these issues, offering potential lessons for the U.S. as it grapples with these challenges.

7. Role of Political Education: Educating citizens about the intricacies of their political system, including the impact of Senate representation and filibustering, is crucial. It helps the public understand these complexities, fostering informed dialogue about potential reforms and encouraging greater participation in the democratic process.

In conclusion, addressing the complexities of disproportionate representation and the 60-Senate-vote threshold requires careful navigation, drawing from lessons in political history, global comparative studies, and active public discourse. It is an ongoing process, central to the evolution and strengthening of democratic institutions.

Chapter 28

The Electoral College: A Disproportionate Representation of the Popular Vote

W: The Electoral College, established by Article II, Section 1, Clause 2 of the U.S. Constitution, is the formal body that elects the President and Vice President of the United States. While it was designed as a compromise between direct election by the citizens and election by Congress, critics argue that the Electoral College often fails to accurately reflect the will of the majority of American voters, leading to a system of disproportionate representation.

The Functioning of the Electoral College

Each state is allocated a set number of electors, equal to the total number of its Senators and Representatives in Congress. The District of Columbia is awarded three electors, bringing the total number of electors to 538. A candidate needs an absolute majority of these electors - at least 270 - to win the presidency.

In most states, a "winner-takes-all" system is in place, where the candidate receiving the majority of the popular vote in a state wins all of that state's electoral votes. However, this means that the votes for the losing candidate(s) in each state are essentially disregarded at the national level.

Misalignment with the Popular Vote

Several instances throughout U.S. history have demonstrated a disconnect between the Electoral College outcome and the popular vote. Five times - in 1824, 1876, 1888, 2000, and 2016 - candidates have won the presidency despite losing the popular vote. This discrepancy raises concerns about the democratic nature of the Electoral College system and whether it truly represents the will of the people.

Disproportionate Representation

A fundamental critique of the Electoral College lies in its allocation of electoral votes, which critics argue leads to disproportionate representation. Less populated states have more electoral power per person than more populous states. This is because the minimum number of electors for any state (three) overrepresents smaller states relative to their population.

For instance, one elector from Wyoming represents about 193,000 people, while one elector from California represents over 700,000 people. This implies that a vote cast in Wyoming has more than three times the impact on the Electoral College than a vote cast in California.

Influence on Campaign Strategies

The Electoral College also impacts campaign strategies, with candidates focusing on "swing states" rather than nationwide campaigns. As a result, the issues and interests of voters in non-competitive states can be sidelined, further undermining the principle of equal representation.

Reform Proposals

The debate on whether to reform or eliminate the Electoral College continues. Some propose replacing it with a direct popular vote, while others suggest a proportional allocation of electoral votes. Regardless of the solution, the goal is to create a more equitable system that better aligns with the principle of "one person, one vote."

Despite its initial intent to balance power and ensure fair representation, the Electoral College, in its current form, has been criticized for failing to accurately mirror the popular vote. This incongruity underscores the need for a comprehensive examination of the system and potential reforms that better reflect the principles of democratic representation.

A: The Electoral College's disproportionate representation of the popular vote has been a subject of ongoing debate and criticism. Here are some additional points to consider:

1. Minority Rule: The Electoral College has the potential to allow a candidate to win the presidency while receiving fewer votes than their opponent, undermining the principle of majority rule. This raises concerns about the legitimacy of election outcomes and whether they truly reflect the will of the people. Critics argue that the system should prioritize the popular vote to ensure a more democratic and representative process.

2. Impact on Voter Participation: The winner-takes-all system employed by most states in the Electoral College can have unintended consequences for voter participation. In solidly red or blue states, voters who align with the minority party may feel their votes have little impact and may be discouraged from participating. This can lead to decreased voter engagement and a sense of disenfranchisement among certain groups.

3. Concentration of Campaign Efforts: The Electoral College influences campaign strategies, leading candidates to concentrate their resources and attention on battleground states where the outcome is uncertain. This can result in candidates

prioritizing the interests and concerns of these states over those of other regions, potentially neglecting the needs of a significant portion of the population.

4. Potential for Electoral Deadlocks: The Electoral College system opens the possibility of electoral deadlocks, where no candidate reaches the required majority of electoral votes. In such cases, the election is decided by the House of Representatives, with each state delegation having one vote. This introduces another layer of complexity and can result in outcomes that do not align with the popular vote or democratic principles.

5. Impact on Representation: The disproportional allocation of electoral votes can result in a skewed representation of the population. Smaller states, with fewer populations, have a disproportionately large influence in the Electoral College. This can lead to situations where the preferences of a minority of the population hold more weight than those of the majority, raising questions about fairness and equal representation.

6. Potential for Reform: The flaws and criticisms surrounding the Electoral College have prompted discussions on potential

reforms. Proposals include the National Popular Vote Interstate Compact, which aims to bypass the Electoral College by awarding states' electoral votes to the winner of the national popular vote. Other proposals suggest amendments to the Constitution to modify or abolish the Electoral College system altogether. These discussions highlight the need for an ongoing examination of the electoral process and the pursuit of reforms that enhance fairness, representativeness, and democratic principles.

In conclusion, the Electoral College's disproportionate representation of the popular vote is a matter of concern in the U.S. political system. As the nation continues to evaluate the principles of fairness, representation, and democratic legitimacy, a critical examination of the Electoral College and potential reforms is essential to ensure a more equitable and representative electoral process.

4: The Electoral College system's divergence from the popular vote has led to considerable debate over its validity and fairness. Here are additional insights to consider:

1. Historical Context: The Founding Fathers established the Electoral College as a safeguard against potential tyranny of the

majority, intending to create a balance of power. They believed direct democracy could be swayed by demagoguery, while election by Congress could infringe upon the separation of powers. Understanding this historical context is important, even as we examine the system's contemporary implications.

2. The "Faithless Elector" Issue: The Electoral College also raises the possibility of "faithless electors" - electors who vote contrary to the popular vote of their state. While rare, such occurrences can further erode trust in the electoral process and contribute to the perception of a democratic deficit.

3. Voting Power Disparities: The Electoral College system, similar to the Senate's structure, amplifies the voting power of less populous states. This can lead to a paradox where a presidential candidate prioritizes issues that aren't necessarily of concern to the majority of Americans but are crucial to winning specific swing states.

4. Socio-Political Impact: The divergence between the Electoral College and the popular vote can also exacerbate socio-

political divisions. Candidates may focus on issues that resonate with voters in swing states, leading to a politics of polarization where national unity takes a backseat to regional interests.

5. The Need for a Deliberative Approach to Reform: Reforming or replacing the Electoral College would require careful consideration of potential unintended consequences. For example, moving to a direct popular vote could shift candidates' focus to highly populous urban areas, possibly neglecting rural voters' concerns.

6. Resilience of the Constitution: The continued debates over the Electoral College also highlight the enduring flexibility of the U.S. Constitution. Its amendment process allows for the possibility of change and adaptation to new democratic norms and expectations.

7. Broader Democratic Dialogue: The Electoral College debate contributes to broader discussions on democracy and representation, engaging citizens in rethinking electoral systems and norms. This dialogue is an integral part of a healthy, vibrant democracy.

In sum, the debate over the Electoral College's perceived disproportionate representation of the popular vote underscores the dynamism and complexity of democratic governance. It opens opportunities for deepening our understanding of democratic principles, evolving electoral norms, and advancing a more inclusive and representative democracy.

Chapter 29

The Impact and Flaws of Special Interest Political Donations

W: In the complex arena of United States politics, special interest donations play a powerful role, often raising questions about the very integrity of our democratic process.

Special interests, encompassing corporations, labor unions, and issue-based organizations, can contribute significant sums of money to political campaigns, political action committees (PACs), and Super PACs. These contributions, often instrumental in funding expensive campaigns, come with an implicit expectation of reciprocity that poses a serious problem.

The potential influence of these donations on politicians' decisions and policy-making could be detrimental to the democratic process. Policy can be skewed to favor those who can afford to donate large sums, effectively giving them more political voice than the average voter. This creates an imbalance of power that undermines the democratic principle of equal representation.

Furthermore, the Supreme Court's Citizens United decision in 2010 exacerbated this issue by allowing corporations and unions to spend unlimited amounts on political campaigns. This has led to an explosion in the amount of money flowing into the political system, much of it from anonymous sources, a phenomenon known as 'dark money'. The public, in turn, lacks the transparency necessary to understand who is influencing their elected officials.

Lastly, an often-overlooked flaw is the potential diversion of politicians' time and energy from public service to fundraising activities. To secure the substantial funds necessary to wage a successful campaign, politicians may find themselves obligated to court donors and engage in constant fundraising, diverting their attention away from their legislative responsibilities.

In conclusion, special interest political donations present a significant flaw in the U.S. political system. They create an imbalance of power, threaten the transparency and integrity of the democratic process, and divert politicians' attention away from public service to fundraising. While campaign finance reform is often proposed as a solution, the specifics are subject to heated debate and a clear path forward has yet to emerge.

A: Special interest political donations and their impact on the democratic process continue to be a subject of concern and debate. Here are some additional points to consider:

1. Influence on Policy Decisions: Special interest donations can lead to a perception, if not a reality, that policy decisions are influenced by the preferences of wealthy donors rather than the needs and interests of the general public. This raises questions about the fairness and integrity of the policymaking process and can erode public trust in the political system.

2. Disproportionate Representation: The ability of special interest groups to contribute significant sums of money to political campaigns can result in unequal representation. Individuals and organizations with substantial financial resources may gain more access to policymakers and have a greater ability to shape the policy agenda, effectively amplifying their influence over those without the means to make substantial donations. This undermines the principle of equal representation and can lead to policies that favor the interests of a few over the broader public.

3. Potential for Corruption: The expectation of reciprocity that often accompanies special interest donations raises concerns about potential corruption. The pressure to cater to the interests of wealthy donors can create a system in which policymakers prioritize the concerns of the privileged few over the needs of the general population. This undermines the democratic ideal of serving the public good and can lead to policies that perpetuate inequality and favor specific industries or groups.

4. Impact on Political Competition: The influx of money from special interest donations can distort political competition. Candidates who lack access to significant funding may struggle to compete effectively, limiting the diversity of voices and ideas in the political arena. This can result in a system where incumbents or candidates with strong financial backing have a significant advantage, making it difficult for new or less well-funded candidates to challenge the status quo.

5. Need for Transparency and Accountability: The rise of "dark money" in politics, fueled by the Citizens United

decision, further compounds concerns about the influence of special interest donations. The ability of individuals and organizations to contribute large sums of money anonymously reduces transparency and accountability in the political process. Without knowing the true sources of campaign funding, the public is deprived of crucial information that could inform their voting decisions and hold elected officials accountable.

Efforts to address the flaws associated with special interest political donations have included calls for campaign finance reform, increased transparency, and stricter regulations on the influence of money in politics. However, reaching a consensus on the most effective solutions remains a challenge, as different perspectives and interests come into play. Nonetheless, the ongoing conversation surrounding the impact of special interest donations is vital to preserving the integrity and fairness of the democratic process.

4: The influence of special interest political donations on U.S. politics and its implications are a contentious issue. Here are additional perspectives and complexities to consider:

1. The Role of Lobbying: While not always synonymous with political donations,

lobbying is another means by which special interest groups exert influence over policy-making. While lobbying can provide valuable expert insight into complex issues, it becomes problematic when it contributes to a system where money equates to political influence, undermining the principles of equal representation.

2. Legal Interpretations: The Citizens United ruling was based on the premise that campaign contributions constitute a form of protected free speech under the First Amendment. This presents a constitutional challenge to campaign finance reform, highlighting the delicate balance between preserving democratic integrity and protecting constitutional rights.

3. Impact on Policy Prioritization: Given the large donations they receive, politicians may be swayed to prioritize the issues of their biggest donors. This may lead to a skewed policy agenda that does not adequately address the needs and concerns of the average citizen.

4. Democratic Disengagement: The influence of special interest donations can lead to public disillusionment with the democratic process. If citizens perceive their interests to be

overlooked in favor of big money, they may disengage from the democratic process, which would further exacerbate the problem of unequal representation.

5. Grassroots Fundraising as a Countermeasure: Recent election cycles have seen a rise in grassroots fundraising, where small individual donations add up to substantial campaign war chests. This trend could be a positive countermeasure against the influence of large special interest donations, providing a means for a broader array of interests to be represented.

6. Regulatory Challenges: While transparency and stricter regulations are often suggested as solutions, the effectiveness of these measures can be hampered by practical enforcement difficulties and potential loopholes.

7. Interconnected Reforms: Addressing the influence of special interest donations may require reforms in interconnected areas such as gerrymandering, voting rights, and public campaign financing, underlining the complex and multifaceted nature of democratic reform.

In essence, special interest political donations, while a longstanding part of U.S. politics, raise significant questions about the fairness and integrity of the democratic process. They challenge us to consider how we balance competing constitutional principles and societal interests, and they underscore the ongoing need for vigilance, dialogue, and reform in the pursuit of a more equitable and representative democracy.

Chapter 30

The Paralysis of Polarization

W: Partisan polarization, one of the most glaring flaws in the United States political system, has created a climate of increasing division and stubbornness. As a significant barrier to progress, this heightened polarization disrupts the flow of healthy democratic dialogue, making it difficult for legislators to find common ground and pass much-needed laws.

Polarization refers to the ideological distance between the Democratic and Republican parties and the individuals who identify with them. Over the past few decades, this distance has widened significantly. While differing opinions and robust debates are crucial to the democratic process, the current level of polarization has escalated to a level that often prohibits effective governance.

Political scientists attribute the growth of this extreme polarization to a variety of factors. These include demographic changes, the rise of partisan media outlets, the gerrymandering of congressional districts, and the influence of money in politics. Regardless of the causes, the result is a system wherein compromise, a cornerstone of effective governance, has become almost anathema.

The implications of polarization are vast. Legislative gridlock, wherein important policy initiatives are stalled or never passed, is a prominent consequence. As each party pushes its own agenda with little willingness to cooperate with the opposition, the government's ability to address critical issues such as healthcare, immigration, climate change, or economic inequality is severely compromised.

Moreover, polarization erodes trust in public institutions and fuels political cynicism. The American public, witnessing constant political battles and a lack of substantial progress, can become disillusioned with the political process. This disillusionment, in turn, can result in lower voter turnout and further exacerbate the problem.

In an era of complex challenges that require nuanced solutions, polarization poses a significant obstacle. The country needs leadership willing to rise above partisan lines, collaborate, and craft comprehensive policies. Without significant changes to reduce polarization, the political system remains at risk of further stagnation and gridlock.

Addressing polarization will require concerted efforts from political leaders, institutions, and citizens. For a more constructive political climate, the United States needs to encourage cross-party collaboration, promote a more balanced media environment, consider electoral reforms that discourage extreme partisanship, and perhaps most importantly, nurture a culture of political engagement and dialogue among citizens that prioritizes shared values and common goals over party labels.

A:

1. The Role of Leadership: Leadership plays a crucial role in addressing and mitigating polarization. Leaders who prioritize finding common ground, fostering dialogue, and seeking bipartisan solutions can help bridge the divide and break the cycle of polarization. Leaders who appeal to the shared values and aspirations of the American people can inspire a sense of unity and purpose, encouraging citizens and legislators to work together towards common goals.

2. Media Landscape and Echo Chambers: The media landscape has contributed to the polarization by providing platforms that cater to specific ideological leanings. With the rise of partisan media outlets and the prevalence of social media echo chambers, individuals can easily isolate themselves in information bubbles that reinforce their

existing beliefs. This reinforces tribalism and makes it harder to find common ground based on shared facts and a shared understanding of the challenges facing the nation.

3. Engaging in Constructive Dialogue: Encouraging and fostering constructive dialogue is crucial to addressing polarization. This requires promoting respectful and open-minded discussions that focus on the merits of ideas rather than personal attacks. Creating spaces where individuals with different perspectives can come together, listen to one another, and work towards understanding and compromise is essential for overcoming the barriers of polarization.

4. Building Trust and Restoring Faith in Institutions: Restoring trust in public institutions is essential to combat polarization. Transparency, accountability, and ethical conduct are key components of rebuilding trust. When the public sees that politicians are genuinely working for the common good and prioritizing the needs of the people over partisan interests, faith in the political process can be restored.

5. Promoting Civic Education and Engagement: Enhancing civic education can play a vital role in combating polarization. By equipping citizens with the knowledge and skills necessary to critically evaluate information, engage in civil discourse, and understand the complexities of political issues, individuals can become more active and informed participants in the democratic process. Promoting civic education from an early age can foster a sense of responsibility, empathy, and an understanding of the importance of compromise and collaboration.

Addressing polarization requires a multi-faceted approach that involves leadership, media literacy, open dialogue, trust-building, and civic engagement. By actively working towards reducing polarization and promoting a more inclusive and constructive political climate, the U.S. can foster a healthier democracy that effectively addresses the needs and challenges of its diverse population.

4: here are some more points worth considering:

1. The Role of Technology: Advances in technology and the rise of social media have dramatically shaped the political landscape, often reinforcing polarization. Algorithms tend to promote content that aligns with a

user's existing views, thereby deepening ideological divides. Policymakers and tech companies need to explore ways to counteract this echo chamber effect, and users should be encouraged to engage with diverse sources of information.

2. Gerrymandering and Electoral Reform: Gerrymandering, or the practice of manipulating electoral district boundaries for political advantage, can amplify polarization by creating "safe" districts that favor one party. It may also incentivize candidates to cater to the more extreme elements of their base. Reforming the redistricting process to ensure fair representation can help reduce extreme partisanship.

3. Campaign Finance: The influence of money in politics can exacerbate polarization. Large campaign contributions may push candidates towards extreme positions that align with their donors, rather than the broader electorate. Campaign finance reform could limit the influence of special interest groups and encourage politicians to appeal to a broader spectrum of voters.

4. Ranked-Choice Voting: Implementing ranked-choice voting, where voters rank

candidates in order of preference rather than voting for a single candidate, can incentivize more moderate stances. Candidates would aim to appeal to a wider range of voters to gain not only first-choice votes but also second and third choices.

5. Encouraging Bipartisan Cooperation: Building institutional structures that encourage bipartisan cooperation can help foster a less polarized political culture. For example, bipartisan committees or task forces focused on key issues could help facilitate dialogue, compromise, and collaborative policy development.

6. Cultivating Civic Virtues: Encouraging civic virtues like tolerance, humility, and a willingness to compromise can help mitigate polarization at the citizen level. Public campaigns, educational programs, and civic organizations can play a role in promoting these values.

Addressing the paralysis of polarization is no easy task, as it is deeply ingrained in the current political system. However, through a combination of policy changes, leadership initiatives, public education, and shifts in social norms, it is possible to make progress towards a more productive and less polarized political climate.

Chapter 31

The Role of Money: Campaign Finance and Lobbying Influence

Section 1: Campaign Finance

W: The American political system is heavily influenced by the role of money, creating substantial challenges and breeding potential improprieties. Although there are limits to campaign contributions from individuals, PACs, and corporations, money's enormous influence in politics remains unabated.

Campaign finance reform has been a perennial issue, with individuals and organizations pushing for stricter controls over the amount of money that can be donated to political candidates and parties. The Supreme Court decision in Citizens United v. FEC in 2010, which ruled that corporations and unions could spend unlimited amounts of money in elections, exacerbated this issue. Critics argue that this decision has led to a further imbalance in political power and has skewed the political process in favor of those with deep pockets.

Moreover, the advent of super PACs (political action committees), capable of raising and spending unlimited amounts of money, has magnified the role of wealthy donors, corporations, and special interest groups in shaping political outcomes. Critics contend that this unduly influences elections and policy-making, potentially leading to corruption and the undermining of democracy.

Section 2: Lobbying Influence

Lobbying, the act of influencing policymakers and legislation, is an integral part of the American political system. However, it is fraught with challenges. Despite being a legitimate tool for interest groups to voice their concerns and inform policy decisions, lobbying can also lead to disproportionate representation and undue influence.

It's often the case that larger, wealthier interest groups can afford more lobbyists and thus have a louder voice in policy discussions. This can lead to a political landscape where the concerns of ordinary citizens are drowned out by the interests of the well-funded and well-connected.

Furthermore, the 'revolving door' phenomenon, where former public officials become lobbyists and vice versa, exacerbates these issues. This situation can lead to conflicts of interest and a perception of an insider's game, damaging public trust in the political system.

Both campaign finance and lobbying highlight structural flaws in the U.S political system. The immense role of money and interest groups in politics can lead to unequal representation and potentially corrupt practices, detracting from the democratic principles of fairness and equality. Comprehensive reform in both areas is needed to balance these influences and ensure a more democratic political process.

A:

1. Disclosure and Transparency: Enhancing disclosure and transparency requirements can help address the influence of money in politics. Requiring timely and comprehensive reporting of campaign contributions and expenditures, as well as disclosing the sources of funding for super PACs and other political entities, can provide voters with vital information about who is supporting candidates and influencing the political process. Increased transparency can help hold politicians accountable and empower voters to make informed decisions.

2. Public Financing of Elections: Exploring and implementing public financing systems for political campaigns can reduce the influence of big money and level the playing field. By

providing candidates with public funds for their campaigns, reliance on private donations and wealthy special interest groups can be diminished. Public financing can encourage more diverse candidates to run for office and ensure that elected officials prioritize the concerns and needs of the broader public rather than catering to the interests of a select few.

3. Strengthening Ethics and Anti-Corruption Measures: Robust ethics and anti-corruption laws are essential to prevent undue influence and maintain the integrity of the political system. Stricter regulations on campaign contributions, lobbying activities, and conflicts of interest can help minimize the risk of corruption and promote a more transparent and accountable political environment. Effective enforcement mechanisms and penalties for violations are also critical to ensure compliance and deter unethical behavior.

4. Empowering Grassroots Movements and Citizen Engagement: Fostering grassroots movements and encouraging active citizen participation can counterbalance the influence of money in politics. When citizens are engaged, informed, and mobilized, they can advocate for their interests and hold

elected officials accountable. Encouraging civic education, facilitating public forums and debates, and supporting community organizing efforts can empower citizens to actively shape the political agenda and demand policies that reflect their concerns and aspirations.

Addressing the role of money in politics and the influence of lobbying requires comprehensive and multifaceted reform efforts. By enhancing transparency, exploring public financing options, strengthening ethics regulations, and promoting citizen engagement, the U.S. can take significant steps towards a more equitable and democratic political system that serves the interests of all citizens, not just the privileged few.

Balanced Lobbying Representation: Addressing lobbying inequalities could involve mechanisms that ensure that public interest groups have equal opportunities to influence policy.

For instance, public funding could support nonprofit advocacy groups that represent issues like public health, environmental protection, or social justice.

This could help level the lobbying field, so policy is not disproportionately influenced by wealthy corporate interests.

4:

1. Citizen Engagement Platforms: Modern technology could help decentralize political influence and promote greater citizen participation. Digital platforms could be developed to allow citizens to engage directly with legislative processes. These might involve everything from discussions on policy to crowdfunding for political campaigns. Such initiatives can help rebalance the political landscape and provide a counterweight to the influence of money in politics.

2. Regulatory Bodies: Strengthening independent regulatory bodies tasked with monitoring and enforcing campaign finance and lobbying rules is crucial. Regulatory bodies need adequate resources and autonomy to carry out their duties effectively. These institutions could play a role in scrutinizing the fundraising practices of politicians, enforcing lobbying rules, and ensuring the accountability of public officials.

3. Limiting the "Revolving Door": Stricter rules could be put in place to limit the "revolving door" phenomenon between public service and lobbying roles. Cooling-off periods

could be mandated, where officials must wait a certain period of time before moving into lobbying roles post-public service. This could help reduce conflicts of interest and the perception of inside dealings.

4. Media's Role: The media also has a significant role in scrutinizing and reporting on the influence of money in politics. Investigative journalism can uncover unethical practices, while clear and accessible reporting on campaign financing and lobbying can educate the public, helping to hold politicians and special interests accountable.

The influence of money in politics is a multifaceted issue with far-reaching impacts on democratic processes. It's clear that a blend of reforms is necessary, addressing campaign financing, lobbying, citizen engagement, and the role of media, in order to encourage a political landscape that truly represents the interests of all citizens.

Chapter 32

The Flaw of Voter Suppression and Limited Access to Voting

W: Voter suppression and limited access to voting represent significant flaws in the U.S. political system. The principle of democracy dictates that every citizen should have equal access to voting. However, certain regulations, both historical and contemporary, can disproportionately hinder some groups from expressing their political will.

Historically, various laws were designed to suppress votes, particularly among minority groups. Techniques like literacy tests, poll taxes, and outright intimidation served to systematically exclude African American voters in many parts of the U.S., particularly in the South.

Modern forms of voter suppression, albeit less overt, can still disproportionately affect marginalized communities. These include strict voter identification laws, the closing of polling places in predominantly minority neighborhoods, purges of voter rolls, and limitations on early and absentee voting.

Voter ID laws, for instance, are often presented as a measure to prevent voter fraud. However, studies have repeatedly shown that voter fraud is exceptionally rare, leading critics to argue that these laws disproportionately affect low-income individuals, racial and ethnic minorities, and the elderly, who may not have the required identification or the means to obtain it.

The closing of polling places can create longer wait times and necessitate more extended travel for voters. These issues are often more severe in urban areas with high minority populations. As a result, many eligible voters may be discouraged, or entirely unable, to vote.

Restrictive voting laws can also disproportionately affect the elderly and people with disabilities, who might have difficulty standing in line for extended periods, traveling to polling places, or even obtaining an ID due to mobility challenges.

Therefore, while it's crucial to maintain the integrity of the voting process, it is equally important that such measures do not unfairly impede certain groups of people from casting their votes.

In a truly democratic system, all eligible citizens should have fair and reasonable access to vote, regardless of their race, socioeconomic status, or physical ability.

A:

1. Racial and Socioeconomic Disparities: Voter suppression measures have historically and disproportionately impacted minority communities and low-income individuals. The legacy of discriminatory practices, such as poll taxes and literacy tests, has had a lasting impact on voting access for marginalized groups. Addressing voter suppression requires acknowledging and remedying these historical inequities to ensure equal participation for all citizens.

2. Disenfranchisement of Incarcerated Individuals: The disenfranchisement of individuals with felony convictions is another aspect of voter suppression that warrants attention. Laws vary across states, with some permanently stripping voting rights from individuals with felony convictions, disproportionately affecting communities of color due to racial disparities in the criminal justice system. Restoring voting rights to formerly incarcerated individuals can promote their reintegration into society and foster a more inclusive democracy.

3. Accessibility for Marginalized Communities: Enhancing accessibility to

voting is crucial to ensure equal participation. Efforts should be made to expand the availability of polling places in underserved areas and provide adequate resources, such as transportation options, to enable individuals to reach polling locations. Additionally, implementing policies that prioritize accessibility for individuals with disabilities, such as providing accessible voting machines and accommodations at polling places, is essential to ensure their full and equal participation in the democratic process.

4. Automatic and Same-Day Voter Registration: Implementing automatic and same-day voter registration can help mitigate the impact of voter suppression. Automatic registration can increase the number of eligible voters by streamlining the registration process and reducing barriers. Same-day registration allows individuals to register and vote on the same day, providing an opportunity for those who may have missed registration deadlines or encountered other obstacles to participate in the election.

5. Education and Outreach: Enhancing civic education and conducting robust voter outreach campaigns can empower citizens

with knowledge about their voting rights, registration procedures, and ways to address potential barriers. Promoting awareness of available resources, such as voter assistance hotlines, can help individuals navigate the voting process and seek assistance if they encounter difficulties or face intimidation.

6. Efforts to combat voter suppression and expand access to voting should be rooted in the principle of ensuring equal representation and eliminating barriers to participation. By addressing historical disparities, improving accessibility, and empowering marginalized communities, the U.S. can work towards a more inclusive and vibrant democracy.

4:

To expand on the points raised:

1. Legal Reforms: Legal action against unjust voting laws and practices can be a critical tool in addressing voter suppression. Organizations and individuals can challenge discriminatory laws in court and advocate for legislation that expands voting access. Legal remedies can be slow and contentious, but they are essential to establish precedents that protect voting rights and encourage more equitable practices.

2. Mail-in and Absentee Voting: Expanding the accessibility of mail-in and absentee voting can also serve as a critical measure against voter suppression. It allows people who may have difficulty reaching polling stations — due to distance, work schedules, health conditions, or other barriers — to vote. While concerns have been raised about potential fraud with mail-in voting, multiple studies suggest that such fraud is extremely rare, and proper safeguards can further minimize risks.

3. Election Day as a National Holiday: Making Election Day a national holiday or placing it on a weekend could boost voter turnout. By eliminating work-related constraints, more citizens may have the opportunity to participate in elections. This could be particularly beneficial to low-income individuals who might otherwise struggle to take time off work to vote.

4. Nonpartisan Redistricting: Voter suppression can also occur through gerrymandering, where electoral district boundaries are drawn in a way that favors one political party. Implementing nonpartisan redistricting can help ensure fair representation and prevent parties from

manipulating electoral boundaries to their advantage.

5. Technological Solutions: The use of technology can offer solutions to enhance voting access and counter suppression tactics. Digital platforms can simplify voter registration, provide accurate information on voting procedures, and offer secure methods for individuals to cast their votes. These initiatives must be paired with robust cybersecurity measures to protect the integrity of the voting process.

6. Vigilance and Active Citizenship: Citizen vigilance plays a key role in countering voter suppression. Being informed about one's rights, reporting irregularities, and participating in civic activities like poll watching can help deter voter suppression activities.

Addressing voter suppression requires a holistic approach that combines legal, legislative, and civic efforts. Each of these components contributes to the larger goal of a truly democratic society, wherein every eligible individual has a fair and equal opportunity to vote.

Wealth Inequality Solutions
Chapter 33

Addressing Wealth Inequality Through Tax Reforms and Regulations

Introduction

W: Wealth inequality has been a longstanding issue in the United States and has seen a sharp increase over the past few decades. To ensure a more equitable distribution of wealth and opportunities, several measures can be undertaken to regulate wealth accumulation. This chapter focuses on four potential solutions aimed at fixing wealth inequality: closing offshore tax havens, imposing a tax on high-value luxury goods, raising the estate tax, and increasing the capital gains tax on high earners.

Section 1: Closing Offshore Tax Havens

Offshore tax havens allow wealthy individuals and corporations to stash assets and earnings in low-tax jurisdictions, significantly reducing their tax liabilities. By closing offshore tax havens, the government can ensure that wealth is not siphoned off without being subject to tax. This would result in increased tax revenues which could be utilized for public welfare programs, ultimately reducing wealth inequality.

Section 2: Taxing High-Value Luxury Goods

Introducing a tax on high-value luxury goods can serve as a means to redistribute wealth. Luxury goods are predominantly purchased by the affluent, so a tax on these items would primarily affect those with higher incomes. Revenue from this tax could be used to fund programs that support lower-income individuals, such as affordable housing, education, and healthcare.

Section 3: Raising the Estate Tax

The estate tax is a tax on the transfer of an estate of a deceased person. By raising the estate tax, it can be ensured that significant wealth is not passed down through generations without being fairly taxed. This can prevent the concentration of wealth within a few families and ensure a more equitable distribution among the population.

Section 4: Increasing Capital Gains Tax on High Earners

Capital gains tax is levied on the profit made from selling an asset. High earners often derive a substantial portion of their income from investments. Raising the capital gains tax on high earners could reduce the disparity between the wealthy, who often have significant investment incomes, and the average wage earner. The revenue generated could be invested in social programs that benefit the wider population.

Conclusion

Wealth inequality is a complex issue that requires a multifaceted approach. Through the implementation of the solutions outlined in this chapter, there is potential to create a more equitable society. By ensuring that the affluent pay their fair share through taxes and that revenues are used to support programs that benefit all citizens, the U.S. can take steps towards reducing wealth inequality.

A:

1. Economic Growth and Incentives: Critics of these tax reforms and regulations argue that they may stifle economic growth and discourage investment. They contend that high taxes on the wealthy and businesses could hinder innovation and entrepreneurship. However, proponents argue that addressing wealth inequality is essential for long-term economic stability and social cohesion. They believe that the benefits of reducing inequality, such as increased consumer spending and social

mobility, can outweigh any potential short-term impacts on economic growth.

2. International Cooperation: Addressing wealth inequality through tax reforms and regulations may require international cooperation. Offshore tax havens, for example, often involve cross-border financial activities. Collaborative efforts between countries to combat tax evasion and enforce transparency in financial transactions are crucial. International agreements and organizations, such as the Organisation for Economic Co-operation and Development (OECD), can play a significant role in facilitating these efforts.

3. Ensuring Fairness and Progressivity: Designing tax reforms and regulations that are fair and progressive is essential. Care must be taken to avoid burdening middle-income earners or discouraging investment and economic activity. A well-designed tax system should consider the ability to pay, ensuring that those with higher incomes contribute proportionally more while not hindering economic productivity.

4. Consideration of Unintended Consequences: Any changes to tax policies and regulations should be carefully evaluated to mitigate

potential unintended consequences. For example, increased estate taxes may have implications for family businesses or farms. A comprehensive analysis of the potential impacts, along with targeted provisions to address specific concerns, is crucial to ensure that the reforms effectively address wealth inequality without unintended negative effects.

5. Complementary Policies: While tax reforms and regulations can play a significant role in addressing wealth inequality, they should be complemented by other policies and initiatives. These may include investments in education and skills development, affordable housing programs, strengthening social safety nets, and promoting inclusive economic growth. A comprehensive approach that combines tax reforms with other measures can yield more sustainable and equitable outcomes.

In conclusion, addressing wealth inequality through tax reforms and regulations requires careful consideration and balancing of various factors. By closing offshore tax havens, imposing taxes on luxury goods, raising the estate tax, and increasing capital gains taxes on high earners, the U.S. can take steps toward a more equitable distribution of wealth. However, it is important to consider potential impacts, ensure fairness, and implement complementary policies to create a comprehensive strategy for reducing wealth inequality and fostering a more inclusive society.

4: Adding to these points, there are several more factors to consider:

1. Political Feasibility: Implementing major tax reforms is often politically contentious. The political feasibility of such reforms will largely depend on the broader political climate, the public's attitude toward wealth redistribution, and the willingness of lawmakers to take potentially unpopular actions. Public awareness campaigns and stakeholder engagement are critical to creating an environment conducive to reform.

2. Tax Evasion and Avoidance: While closing tax loopholes and tightening regulations can curb tax evasion, new methods of evasion may emerge. Therefore, continuous monitoring and adjusting of tax regulations is required to ensure their effectiveness over time. Implementing strict penalties for tax evasion and providing adequate resources for enforcement bodies are also essential.

3. Global Tax Competition: In an increasingly globalized world, countries often compete

with each other to attract businesses by offering attractive tax conditions. This can limit the effectiveness of national-level reforms aimed at increasing the tax burden on the wealthy. Greater international cooperation and alignment on tax standards could help counteract this.

4. Impact on Income Mobility: While the measures discussed are aimed at addressing wealth inequality, they could also potentially impact income mobility. For instance, high estate taxes could prevent the accumulation of generational wealth, but they might also make it more challenging for families to move up the wealth ladder. Careful calibration of tax rates is necessary to strike a balance.

5. Socioeconomic Context: Different measures may be more or less effective depending on the specific socioeconomic context. For example, in a society where the majority of wealth is held in property or other physical assets, taxes on high-value luxury goods may be less impactful than estate or capital gains taxes. A nuanced understanding of wealth distribution and its sources is necessary to design effective tax policies.

Addressing wealth inequality through tax reforms and regulations is a complex but essential task. It requires a multifaceted approach, taking into account both the potential impacts of reforms on economic growth and investment, and the need for equity and social justice. With a nuanced understanding of wealth distribution and a commitment to progressive reforms, it is possible to create a more equitable society.

Chapter 34

Leveraging Tax Policies to Address Wealth Inequality

Introduction

W: Wealth inequality has been a long-standing issue in the United States, and it has grown significantly over the past few decades. While there are many contributing factors, tax policies can play a critical role in narrowing the wealth gap. This chapter focuses on two such policies: establishing a wealth tax and making the income tax system more progressive.

Section 1: Establishing a Wealth Tax

Definition and Mechanism:

A wealth tax is a levy on the total value of personal assets, including bank deposits, real estate, assets in insurance, and pension plans, ownership of unincorporated businesses, financial securities, and personal trusts. It aims at redistributing wealth by taxing the rich a small percentage of their net worth.

Benefits:

1. Revenue Generation: A wealth tax could generate substantial revenue, which can be utilized for social programs targeting the less privileged.

2. Reducing Wealth Concentration: By taking a fraction of the wealthiest individuals' wealth, it reduces the concentration of wealth and fosters a more equitable society.

Challenges:

- Implementation: It might be challenging to assess the value of non-liquid assets accurately.

- Capital Flight: Wealthy individuals might move their assets abroad to evade wealth tax.

Section 2: Making the Income Tax System More Progressive

Definition and Mechanism:

A progressive income tax system is one where the tax rate increases as the taxable amount increases. This means that high-income earners pay a larger percentage of their income in taxes compared to those with lower incomes.

Benefits:

- Fairness: It is based on the ability to pay. Those who earn more can afford to pay a higher percentage of their income in taxes.
- Reducing Income Inequality: By taking a larger percentage from the higher-income groups, it helps reduce income inequality.

Challenges:

- Economic Disincentive: Critics argue that too high tax rates for the wealthy can create disincentives for entrepreneurship and investment.
- Complexity: A progressive system can be more complicated due to varying tax brackets and rules.

Conclusion

Both establishing a wealth tax and making the income tax system more progressive are viable solutions to address wealth inequality. It is crucial for policymakers to carefully evaluate and implement tax reforms aimed at reducing wealth inequality while fostering economic growth and stability.

A:

1. Administrative Challenges: Implementing a wealth tax and making the income tax

system more progressive require effective administration and enforcement. Proper mechanisms must be in place to accurately assess wealth, especially for non-liquid assets, and to ensure compliance. Adequate resources and expertise within tax authorities are essential for the successful implementation of these policies.

2. International Considerations: Wealth taxation can pose challenges when it comes to international mobility of capital and individuals. To avoid capital flight or individuals relocating to countries with more favorable tax regimes, coordination and cooperation among nations are necessary. International tax agreements and measures to combat tax evasion and avoidance can help ensure that wealth taxation is effective and equitable.

3. Balancing Incentives and Fairness: Critics of progressive tax policies argue that excessively high tax rates for the wealthy may discourage investment, innovation, and entrepreneurship. It is important to strike a balance between promoting economic growth and ensuring a fair distribution of wealth. Designing tax policies that consider these factors can help create an environment

that encourages economic activity while addressing wealth inequality.

4. Evaluating Redistribution Impact: Implementing tax policies aimed at reducing wealth inequality should be accompanied by rigorous evaluation of their effectiveness. Assessing the impact on wealth distribution, economic growth, and overall societal well-being is crucial to fine-tune policies and ensure that the intended goals are being achieved. Regular monitoring and adjustments may be necessary to optimize outcomes.

5. Complementary Measures: Tax policies alone may not be sufficient to fully address wealth inequality. Complementary measures such as investments in education, job creation, social safety nets, and affordable housing can help provide opportunities and promote upward mobility. A comprehensive approach that combines tax reforms with other strategies can create a more holistic solution to wealth inequality.

In conclusion, leveraging tax policies to address wealth inequality requires careful consideration of administrative challenges, international implications, and the balance between incentives and fairness. By implementing a wealth tax and making the income tax system more progressive, policymakers can take significant steps toward narrowing the wealth gap. Regular evaluation, international cooperation, and complementary measures will be crucial in creating a fairer and more equitable society.

4:

Further to these thoughts, a few additional points to consider are:

1. Political Challenges: Much like any significant policy change, implementing new tax policies will likely face political hurdles. Interest groups, public opinion, and political ideology can all impact the ability to enact these changes. Therefore, political strategy and public engagement will be crucial components of any plan to reform tax policies.

2. Wealth Tax vs. Capital Gains: An alternative to the wealth tax that has been proposed is a more aggressive taxation of capital gains, particularly those derived from the sale of long-held assets or inheritance. This could address some of the issues related to assessing the value of non-liquid assets. However, it also brings its own complexities, such as deciding on a fair rate and

determining exactly when these taxes should be levied.

3. Economic Impact: While progressive income taxes are generally seen as promoting fairness, it's also important to consider their potential impact on the economy. Higher taxes on the wealthy could potentially slow investment and business growth, affecting job creation. Careful calibration of tax rates is necessary to strike a balance between wealth redistribution and economic growth.

4. Perception of Fairness: The concept of fairness in taxation is subjective and can vary widely among the population. While some view progressive taxation and wealth taxes as necessary for fairness, others may see them as punitive towards the wealthy. Policymakers need to consider these perceptions and address them in their communication strategy when proposing and implementing these reforms.

5. Broader Fiscal Policy: Finally, any changes to tax policy should be considered within the context of broader fiscal policy. It's important to examine how these changes align with other fiscal measures such as government spending, debt, and deficit management.

Addressing wealth inequality is a complex task that will likely require a multifaceted approach. While changes to tax policies, like establishing a wealth tax and making the income tax system more progressive, are part of the solution, they need to be combined with other strategies and thoroughly analyzed to ensure they effectively address the issue without causing unintended consequences.

Chapter 35

Addressing Wealth Inequality Through Revenue Tax on Sales in the US

Introduction to Revenue Tax

W: One of the proposed mechanisms to address wealth inequality is the implementation of a revenue tax on all sales generated within the United States, paid by companies. This tax would be levied on the revenue generated from sales, rather than on profits. By targeting revenue, this approach aims to circumvent various tax avoidance strategies employed by corporations and thus contribute to reducing wealth inequality.

Advantages of Tax on Revenue

1. Curtailing Profit Shifting and Tax Avoidance

One of the primary advantages of imposing a tax on revenue is that it mitigates the ability of companies to avoid taxes by shifting profits to other locations. With a focus on sales revenue generated within the United States, there is little room for maneuvering as the tax is levied regardless of where the company might transfer its profits.

2. Reducing Loopholes

Revenue-based taxes tend to have fewer loopholes compared to profit-based taxes. This is because revenue is a more straightforward figure, while profits can be manipulated through deductions, credits, and other accounting practices. With less complexity and fewer variables involved in calculating revenue, there is less opportunity for exploiting gaps in the tax code.

3. Counteracting the Effect of Tax Havens

One common tax avoidance strategy is the use of offshore tax havens. By shifting profits to countries with lower tax rates, corporations can substantially reduce their tax liabilities. However, a revenue tax on sales generated in the US negates this tactic as it is imposed at the point of revenue generation, irrespective of where the profits might later be allocated.

4. Potential for Increased Tax Revenue

Because it's harder to evade and exploit, a revenue tax could increase the overall tax revenue collected from corporations. This additional revenue could be used to fund public services and programs aimed at reducing wealth inequality.

Caveats and Considerations

While the revenue tax has distinct advantages, it is essential to consider the potential repercussions. It's crucial to carefully calibrate the tax rate to ensure that it does not disproportionately affect businesses with lower profit margins. Further, it is necessary to thoroughly evaluate and address any unintended consequences on the broader economy.

Conclusion

A revenue tax on sales generated in the US presents an innovative approach to addressing wealth inequality by ensuring that corporations contribute their fair share. By limiting profit-shifting, reducing loopholes, and counteracting tax havens, this tax could be a significant step towards a more equitable distribution of wealth. However, careful planning and execution are essential to balance the benefits with any potential economic impacts.

A:

1. Economic Impact: Implementing a revenue tax on sales requires a careful analysis of its potential economic impact. It is important to consider how businesses may respond to such a tax, as it could potentially affect their pricing strategies, investment decisions, and overall competitiveness. Assessing the potential consequences on economic growth, employment, and consumer behavior is crucial to strike a balance between reducing wealth inequality and fostering a healthy business environment.

2. International Competitiveness: The implementation of a revenue tax should also take into account the global competitiveness of US businesses. It is important to consider how this tax might affect their ability to compete with companies from other countries that do not have similar tax measures in place. Balancing the objective of reducing wealth inequality with maintaining a favorable business environment and international competitiveness is a delicate task.

3. Administrative Feasibility: The practical implementation of a revenue tax on sales requires a robust administrative framework. This includes ensuring accurate reporting and enforcement mechanisms to prevent tax evasion and ensure compliance. Investing in the necessary resources and infrastructure to effectively administer and enforce this tax is essential for its success.

4. Holistic Approach: While a revenue tax on sales can be a valuable tool in addressing wealth inequality, it is important to recognize that it is not a comprehensive solution on its own. Combining it with other measures, such as progressive income taxation, targeted social policies, and investments in education and social

mobility, can create a more comprehensive approach to reducing wealth inequality.

5. Stakeholder Engagement: The implementation of a revenue tax on sales should involve meaningful dialogue and consultation with various stakeholders, including businesses, economists, policymakers, and the public. Engaging with these stakeholders can help ensure that the tax is designed and implemented in a manner that is fair, effective, and sustainable.

In conclusion, a revenue tax on sales is a promising mechanism for addressing wealth inequality by targeting corporate revenue and reducing tax avoidance strategies. However, careful consideration of economic impacts, international competitiveness, administrative feasibility, and the need for a holistic approach is essential for successful implementation. Engaging stakeholders in the process can help foster support and contribute to the development of a tax policy that promotes both equity and economic growth.

4: Adding to the points above, these considerations might also be significant in the context of implementing a revenue tax on sales:

1. Differential Impacts: Depending on their business model, some industries might be

more heavily impacted by a revenue tax than others. For instance, high-revenue, low-margin businesses such as retail could potentially be hit harder than high-margin businesses like technology companies. Policymakers will need to consider these differences and how they may impact various sectors of the economy.

2. Economic Cycles: The impact of a revenue tax on businesses could also vary depending on economic cycles. In times of economic contraction, a tax on revenue might be more burdensome as companies may still need to pay the tax even if they're not profitable. This could have implications for business solvency and employment during economic downturns.

3. Tax Incidence: While a revenue tax is paid by companies, the economic burden of the tax might be passed on to consumers in the form of higher prices, employees in the form of lower wages, or shareholders in the form of lower returns. The true incidence of the tax, therefore, might still fall on individuals rather than corporations.

4. Legal Challenges: A shift to a revenue tax may face legal challenges, especially if it's seen as punitive or unfairly targeting specific

companies or industries. To ensure the legality and constitutionality of the tax, lawmakers will need to carefully design the policy to withstand potential legal scrutiny.

5. Trade Agreements: Finally, implementing a tax based on sales generated within the US might have implications for international trade agreements. Policymakers will need to ensure that any new tax policies align with existing trade agreements and international tax laws.

In conclusion, while a revenue tax on sales can be an effective tool for addressing wealth inequality, it requires careful consideration of potential impacts on businesses, economic cycles, tax incidence, and legal and international trade considerations. A nuanced understanding of these factors, alongside rigorous analysis and stakeholder consultation, will be crucial in crafting a tax policy that is both effective in reducing inequality and supportive of economic stability and growth.

Chapter 36

Universal Basic Income as a Solution to Wealth Inequality

Introduction to Universal Basic Income

W: Universal Basic Income (UBI), often simply referred to as basic income, is a policy where all citizens of a country receive a regular, unconditional sum of money from the government. This income is provided regardless of employment status or wealth, aiming to guarantee a minimum standard of living for all members of society.

Addressing Wealth Inequality through UBI

Economic Security

One of the primary goals of UBI is to provide economic security. With a guaranteed income, individuals who are unemployed, underemployed, or unable to work due to disabilities, can still maintain a basic standard of living. This effectively reduces poverty levels, which is one of the aspects of wealth inequality.

Encouraging Entrepreneurship and Innovation

Another advantage of UBI is that it can foster entrepreneurship and innovation. When people are not solely dependent on employment for their livelihood, they may be more likely to pursue entrepreneurial endeavors or engage in creative pursuits, which can contribute to economic growth and potentially help redistribute wealth.

Simplifying Welfare Programs

Universal Basic Income can also serve as a replacement for various welfare programs. This simplification can make the social safety net more accessible and reduce the bureaucratic overhead associated with traditional welfare systems. In doing so, it ensures that more financial resources directly reach the individuals who need them most.

Flexibility in the Labor Market

UBI offers individuals greater flexibility in the labor market. With a guaranteed income, people can afford to be more selective in the jobs they accept. This can lead to a better match between employees' skills and job requirements, potentially increasing productivity and wages, which can mitigate wealth inequality to some extent.

Redistribution of Wealth

By funding UBI through progressive taxation, where the wealthy are taxed at higher rates, wealth can be effectively redistributed. This ensures that those at the lower end of the income spectrum receive a larger share of the nation's wealth, helping to narrow the wealth gap.

Potential Challenges

While UBI has the potential to address wealth inequality, it's essential to consider the possible challenges and criticisms. These include the high costs associated with implementing UBI, potential inflationary effects, and concerns about discouraging work.

Conclusion

Universal Basic Income represents a bold and potentially transformative policy to address wealth inequality. By providing all citizens with a basic income, it can alleviate poverty, encourage innovation, and facilitate wealth redistribution. However, careful consideration of the implementation details and potential challenges is crucial for the success of such a policy.

A:

1. Cost Considerations: Implementing a Universal Basic Income would require

substantial financial resources. The costs associated with providing a basic income to every citizen need to be carefully evaluated and balanced against other government priorities. Funding mechanisms, such as progressive taxation, may need to be implemented to ensure the sustainability and affordability of UBI.

2. Behavioral and Work Incentives: Critics of UBI argue that providing a guaranteed income might disincentivize work and lead to a decline in productivity. Careful design and consideration of the policy's impact on work incentives are necessary to strike a balance between providing economic security and encouraging labor force participation.

3. Impact on Social Programs: UBI has the potential to simplify the welfare system by replacing existing social programs. However, transitioning from the current system to UBI requires careful planning and consideration to ensure that vulnerable populations continue to receive the necessary support and services.

4. Potential for Social and Economic Transformation: UBI has the potential to create a more equitable society by

addressing wealth inequality. It can empower individuals to make choices based on their aspirations, creativity, and personal development rather than solely on financial constraints. This transformation may require changes in societal attitudes and structures to fully realize the benefits of UBI.

5. Long-Term Effects: Implementing UBI requires a long-term perspective. It is important to monitor and evaluate the effects of UBI on wealth inequality, poverty rates, labor market dynamics, and overall societal well-being. Adjustments and fine-tuning of the policy may be necessary to ensure its effectiveness and adaptability to changing economic and social circumstances.

In conclusion, Universal Basic Income has the potential to be a transformative policy in addressing wealth inequality. By providing a basic income to all citizens, it can ensure economic security, encourage entrepreneurship, and redistribute wealth. However, the challenges associated with implementation, funding, work incentives, and the broader socioeconomic impact require careful consideration and continuous evaluation. A well-designed and well-implemented UBI policy can contribute to a more equitable and inclusive society.

4: Complementing the above points, the following considerations should also be taken into account when discussing Universal Basic Income (UBI) as a tool for addressing wealth inequality:

1. Income vs. Wealth: UBI primarily addresses income inequality by providing everyone with a guaranteed income. However, wealth inequality, which considers assets owned minus debts, is a separate but related issue. While UBI can help with the income aspect, complementary policies addressing wealth accumulation (e.g., taxes on wealth or capital gains) might also be necessary to fully tackle wealth inequality.

2. Political Acceptability: The implementation of UBI is not just an economic issue but a political one. Convincing lawmakers and the public of its merits and affordability may be challenging, especially in societies that emphasize the link between work and income. A shift in societal norms and values may be necessary for UBI to be politically viable.

3. Potential Inflation: There are concerns that UBI could cause inflation, as it may increase the demand for goods and services without a corresponding increase in supply. Policymakers need to take into account this

potential impact on the cost of living, which could undermine the goal of reducing poverty and inequality.

4. Effects on Different Demographics: The impact of UBI could vary across different demographics, and it's important to consider these differences. For instance, it could disproportionately benefit groups who have been systemically disadvantaged in the labor market, such as women, racial and ethnic minorities, and people with disabilities.

5. Universal vs. Targeted Approach: UBI is a universal program, which means it benefits everyone, including the wealthy. An alternative approach could be a negative income tax, where payments are targeted to those below a certain income level. This could be more cost-effective in reducing poverty and inequality, although it loses some of the simplicity and stigma-free advantages of UBI.

In conclusion, while UBI has potential as a tool for addressing income inequality and providing a safety net for all citizens, it's essential to take into account the broader implications. These include its interaction with wealth inequality, political feasibility, potential inflationary effects, differential impacts on various demographics, and the trade-offs between a universal and targeted approach. A comprehensive and nuanced understanding of these issues is key to designing a UBI policy that is both effective and sustainable.

Chapter 37

Certified Companies as a Solution to Wealth Inequality

Introduction

W: Wealth inequality remains one of the most pressing challenges of our time. As corporations amass more wealth, the gap between the rich and the poor continues to widen. A potential solution that can help bridge this gap is the concept of Certified Companies.

Certified Companies: An Overview

The central idea behind Certified Companies is to incentivize corporations to adopt practices that foster a fairer distribution of wealth, sustainability, and worker representation. Companies that meet specific criteria can become "Certified" and enjoy a reduced corporate tax rate of 10%. Those that do not comply would pay a higher rate of 28%.

Criteria for Certification

1. Employee Representation on the Board: 20% of the company's board must be elected by the employees. This ensures that the workforce has a voice in decision-making

processes, potentially leading to decisions that consider the well-being of all stakeholders.

2. Union Requirement: The company must establish a union, which will be run by the board members elected by the employees. Unions play a significant role in ensuring fair wages and better working conditions.

3. Environmental Responsibility: The company must achieve carbon neutrality, thereby contributing to the fight against climate change.

4. Executive Pay Ratio Cap: There must be a cap on the ratio of top executive pay to worker pay. This ensures that the executives do not receive disproportionately high compensation compared to the average worker, contributing to a fairer wealth distribution.

Potential Benefits

Enhanced Worker Representation

By ensuring that employees have representation on the board, Certified Companies can foster an environment where decisions are made with the welfare of the entire company in mind, rather than just the executives.

Encouraging Sustainable Practices

Requiring companies to be carbon neutral as part of the certification incentivizes them to adopt sustainable practices, which is beneficial for society as a whole.

Addressing Wealth Inequality

The executive pay ratio cap can ensure a more equitable distribution of company profits, which can contribute to reducing wealth inequality.

A More Competitive and Responsible Corporate Sector

Lower tax rates for Certified Companies could drive corporations to adopt more responsible and sustainable practices in order to qualify for the certification.

Conclusion

The Certified Companies model represents an innovative approach to encouraging corporate practices that can contribute to reducing wealth inequality, promoting sustainability, and ensuring employee representation. Through a combination of tax incentives and specific criteria, it aligns corporate interests with broader societal goals.

A:

1. Encouraging Responsible Corporate Behavior: The Certified Companies model

incentivizes corporations to adopt responsible practices by linking their tax rates to specific criteria. By promoting worker representation, environmental responsibility, and fair wealth distribution, companies are encouraged to prioritize broader societal interests alongside profit-making.

2. Potential Impact on Economic Equality: The requirement for employee representation on the board and the executive pay ratio cap can contribute to a more equitable distribution of wealth within companies. This can help address the wealth gap between executives and workers, promoting economic equality and fairness.

3. Balancing Corporate Competitiveness: While the reduced tax rate for Certified Companies can incentivize responsible practices, it is important to ensure that it does not disproportionately disadvantage companies that may struggle to meet the certification criteria. Striking a balance between competitiveness and responsible behavior is crucial to maintain a thriving business environment.

4. Scaling and Widespread Adoption: For the Certified Companies model to have a

significant impact on wealth inequality, widespread adoption is necessary. This requires careful consideration of the scalability and implementation challenges, as well as support from governments, businesses, and other stakeholders.

5. Evaluation and Continuous Improvement: Monitoring the effectiveness of Certified Companies in addressing wealth inequality is essential. Regular assessments and adjustments to the certification criteria can ensure that the model remains relevant and impactful over time. Evaluation should encompass not only the economic impact but also social and environmental outcomes.

In conclusion, the Certified Companies model offers an innovative approach to promote responsible corporate behavior and address wealth inequality. By aligning corporate practices with societal goals and providing tax incentives, it incentivizes companies to prioritize the well-being of their employees, the environment, and the equitable distribution of wealth. Careful consideration, evaluation, and widespread adoption are key to realizing the potential of this model in fostering a more inclusive and fair economy.

4: Beyond the given points, there are additional layers to explore when contemplating the Certified

Companies model as a potential solution to wealth inequality.

1. Incentivization and Market Forces: One central question is whether the proposed tax benefits would be enough to incentivize companies to make the necessary changes for certification. While a lower tax rate is attractive, corporations may also weigh up costs associated with implementing the certification criteria, such as transforming operational processes to become carbon-neutral. Therefore, the Certified Companies model needs to account for varying operational complexities across different industries.

2. Potential Impact on Small and Medium Enterprises: It's crucial to consider the impact of the Certified Companies model on smaller businesses. The certification criteria could be challenging for small and medium enterprises (SMEs) to meet due to limited resources. A tiered or scaled approach might be necessary to ensure that all businesses, regardless of size, can participate and benefit.

3. Legislation and Policy: Implementing a Certified Companies model will require legislative support. Policymakers will need

to create robust and clear guidelines to prevent loopholes that could be exploited. Further, the impact of such policies on international trade and relations should be assessed, as they could influence decisions of multinational corporations.

4. Oversight and Transparency: The success of the Certified Companies model will heavily rely on effective oversight and transparency mechanisms. Independent audits and regular public reporting can ensure that corporations are genuinely meeting the criteria, as opposed to engaging in superficial or short-term changes for certification.

5. Societal Impact: Lastly, while the primary focus is wealth inequality, the societal impact of this model could be far-reaching. Enhanced employee representation could lead to improved worker satisfaction and productivity. Increased environmental responsibility could help combat climate change. These broader benefits should be part of the conversation about Certified Companies.

In conclusion, while the Certified Companies model holds promise for addressing wealth inequality and encouraging responsible corporate behavior, its implementation would require careful consideration of market dynamics, SMEs' needs, legislative and oversight frameworks, and the broad societal impact. It represents a potential shift towards a new paradigm of corporate responsibility, where companies are recognized and rewarded for their contributions to a fairer and more sustainable society.

Political System Solutions

Chapter 38

Advocating for Single-Term Presidency and Addressing Short-Term Thinking in the U.S. Political System

Section 1: A Case for Single-Term Presidency

W: One distinctive feature of the United States political system is the term limit on the presidency. The 22nd Amendment to the U.S. Constitution allows a President to serve up to two terms in office. This approach was designed to prevent the consolidation of power and ward off potential autocracy. However, it can unintentionally contribute to a significant flaw in the system: the constant need for re-election and its impact on policy-making.

A strong argument can be made in favor of transitioning to a single-term presidency. This change would remove the distraction of re-election campaigns and allow Presidents to focus solely on governance. Without the pressure of securing votes for a second term, the President would be free to act in the best interest of the American people throughout their tenure.

This shift could potentially lead to more effective and less partisan decision-making. A President not burdened by electoral concerns could make tough but necessary decisions, addressing critical long-term challenges without fear of political repercussions.

Section 2: Addressing Short-Term Thinking

Despite its merits, a single-term presidency alone would not fully resolve the systemic issue of short-term thinking in U.S. politics. This problem is not exclusive to the presidency but pervades the entire political system. Legislation and policies often align more with short-term objectives connected to election cycles, rather than the nation's long-term interests.

Such an approach can severely hinder comprehensive reforms that require longer timeframes for implementation and to yield results. Issues like climate change, infrastructure development, and social security reform are often relegated to the back burner because they do not offer immediate political gains, despite their critical importance to the nation's future.

Therefore, to complement a single-term presidency, other measures should be considered to promote long-term thinking. These could include extending the terms of congressional representatives or introducing legislative frameworks that prioritize long-term policy goals.

Overall, a shift towards a single-term presidency, coupled with other reforms to promote long-term thinking, could potentially lead to more stable and future-oriented governance, effectively serving the interests of the American people.

A: Continuity and Experience: One potential concern with a single-term presidency is the loss of continuity and institutional memory that can come with limited time in office. Longer presidential terms can allow for a more sustained focus on policy implementation and learning from previous experiences. Without the prospect of re-election, some argue that a President may be less inclined to invest time and effort into building relationships with foreign leaders or engaging in long-term strategic planning.

1. Transition Period and Accountability: Implementing a single-term presidency would require careful consideration of the transition period between administrations. With no opportunity for re-election, Presidents might be seen as "lame ducks"

early in their term, potentially diminishing their effectiveness and authority. Additionally, the absence of a re-election mechanism could raise questions about accountability and checks on executive power. The prospect of a President facing another election can serve as a form of accountability, allowing voters to express approval or disapproval of their performance.

2. Institutional Checks and Balances: While a single-term presidency may mitigate the short-term thinking associated with re-election campaigns, it is important to recognize that other branches of government, such as Congress and the judiciary, also play significant roles in shaping policy and promoting long-term thinking. Strengthening the checks and balances among these branches, as well as enhancing the role of independent advisory bodies, can further address the issue of short-termism in the political system.

3. Public Engagement and Education: In order to foster a political climate that values long-term thinking, there is a need for greater public engagement and education on policy issues and their long-term implications. This can help shift the focus of voters and

politicians alike from short-term gains to more sustainable solutions. Encouraging civic participation, promoting media literacy, and supporting a well-informed electorate are essential components of fostering long-term thinking in the political sphere.

While transitioning to a single-term presidency could be a step towards addressing short-term thinking in U.S. politics, it is important to consider the broader context and potential challenges associated with such a change. A comprehensive approach that includes a range of reforms and promotes a culture of long-term decision-making would be necessary to effectively tackle this systemic issue.

4: Here are a few additional perspectives to consider when discussing a single-term presidency and short-term thinking in U.S. politics:

1. Reduced Partisanship: With no re-election campaign to wage, a single-term President might be less beholden to the extremes of their political party and could govern more from the center. This could potentially reduce partisanship and foster more bipartisan cooperation in addressing critical issues.

2. Balancing Experience and Fresh Perspectives: While a single-term presidency may result in a loss of continuity, it could also mean regular infusion of new perspectives into the White House. The trade-off between experience and fresh ideas is a crucial aspect to consider in this debate.

3. Broadening the Talent Pool: If the presidency were a single-term position, it might attract a wider array of experienced candidates who are otherwise disinclined to commit to a potential eight-year tenure. This could diversify the talent pool and bring fresh leadership to the country more frequently.

4. Longer Terms for Congressional Representatives: Extending the terms of congressional representatives could help balance out the shorter tenure of a single-term President. This could provide more continuity, while also encouraging long-term thinking among lawmakers.

5. Changing the Electoral Cycle: Instead of a four-year single term, the U.S. could consider a six-year or even eight-year single term, akin to some other democracies. This could give the President sufficient time to implement long-term policies while

removing the distraction of re-election campaigns.

6. Public Sector Reform: It might also be beneficial to institute reforms aimed at promoting long-term thinking and stability within the civil service. A professional and efficient public sector can ensure the successful implementation of long-term policies, regardless of political changes.

7. Encouraging Long-term Policy Development: Independent of any changes to term limits, fostering a culture of long-term policy planning, perhaps through the creation of dedicated think-tanks or the promotion of "futures thinking" in government, could be a valuable step towards combating short-termism.

It's important to remember that shifting to a single-term presidency would represent a fundamental change to the U.S. political system, and the potential impacts would need to be considered carefully. However, by fostering an environment conducive to long-term policy-making, it may be possible to strike a balance between stability and innovation, ultimately serving the best interests of the American people.

Chapter 39

Remedying Flaws in the U.S. Political System: The Roles of Ranked-Choice Voting and Independent Redistricting Commissions

W:While the U.S. political system is fraught with flaws, it's important to remember that potential solutions exist, capable of tackling these issues head-on. Two such proposed measures, Ranked-Choice Voting and Independent Redistricting Commissions, merit a closer examination.

Section 1: Ranked-Choice Voting

Ranked-Choice Voting (RCV) is one innovative solution that could greatly improve the democratic process in America. This voting method allows voters to rank candidates in order of preference, thereby providing a more nuanced expression of voter sentiment than the current winner-takes-all system. If a candidate receives more than half of the first-preference votes, they win outright. If not, the candidate with the fewest votes is eliminated, and their votes are reallocated based on second preferences. This process repeats until a candidate garners over half of the active votes.

Ranked-Choice Voting is designed to combat the two-party system's dominance, as it significantly improves third-party and independent candidates' ability to compete. Under the current voting system, these candidates often struggle to gain traction due to fears of "spoiling" an election – the concern that voting for a third-party candidate might inadvertently aid the voter's least preferred candidate. However, with RCV, voters can confidently vote their conscience without risking a spoiler effect, as their vote will default to their second choice if their first choice is eliminated.

Section 2: Independent Redistricting Commissions

Another potential solution to one of the U.S. political system's most persistent flaws – gerrymandering – is the formation of independent redistricting commissions. These non-partisan entities could be responsible for drawing voting district boundaries, thereby diminishing politicians' ability to manipulate electoral maps to their advantage.

Current redistricting processes are often left to legislators, which can lead to partisan gerrymandering, wherein electoral maps are rigged to favor one political party disproportionately. Independent redistricting commissions, composed of non-political experts and citizens, could bring transparency and impartiality to this process. This method is already used in several states, including California and Arizona, and has resulted in more competitive elections and fairer representation.

Both Ranked-Choice Voting and Independent Redistricting Commissions represent viable approaches to tackling inherent flaws in the U.S. political system. If implemented broadly, they have the potential to foster a more equitable, democratic political landscape, that truly reflects the will of the American populace.

A:

1. Enhanced Representation: Ranked-Choice Voting promotes greater representation and diversity in the political landscape. By removing the fear of wasted votes, voters are empowered to support candidates who align more closely with their values, including third-party and independent candidates. This can lead to a broader range of voices being heard and considered in the political decision-making process.

2. Fostering Collaboration and Reducing Polarization: Ranked-Choice Voting encourages candidates to appeal to a wider base of voters, as they seek to be ranked higher on the preference list. This can

incentivize candidates to campaign on a platform of collaboration and consensus-building, rather than relying solely on divisive tactics that cater to a narrow partisan base. As a result, RCV has the potential to mitigate polarization and encourage more constructive dialogue among political actors.

3. Transparency and Fairness: Independent Redistricting Commissions bring transparency and fairness to the redistricting process, as they are designed to operate outside of partisan influence. By removing politicians' direct control over redistricting, these commissions can help alleviate concerns of gerrymandering and ensure that district boundaries are drawn in a manner that reflects the actual communities and their interests, rather than political calculations.

4. Restoring Trust and Confidence: Implementing Ranked-Choice Voting and Independent Redistricting Commissions can help restore trust and confidence in the political system. By addressing the flaws that contribute to voter disillusionment, such as limited choices and manipulated district lines, these reforms can demonstrate a commitment to a fair and inclusive democracy. This, in turn, may encourage

greater civic participation and engagement among the electorate.

5. Adoption and Expansion: While Ranked-Choice Voting and Independent Redistricting Commissions have gained traction in some states, broader adoption and expansion of these reforms across the country would be necessary to maximize their impact. Advocacy for these measures at the state and federal levels, coupled with public education on their benefits, can help garner support and momentum for their implementation nationwide.

It's important to recognize that these reforms are not a panacea and may require careful implementation and ongoing evaluation. However, they offer promising pathways to address key flaws in the U.S. political system, promoting fair representation, collaboration, transparency, and public trust. Through a combination of legislative action, public engagement, and continued exploration of innovative solutions, the U.S. can work towards a more robust and responsive democracy.

4:To provide further commentary on these aspects:

1. Greater Voter Satisfaction: Research on Ranked-Choice Voting (RCV) has shown that it can lead to higher voter satisfaction. By enabling voters to rank their choices, they

have the opportunity to express support for more candidates, which may provide a sense of greater participation in the democratic process. Moreover, since the elected candidate needs to appeal to a broader spectrum of voters to secure preference rankings, it can result in elected officials who better represent their constituents' views.

2. Lowering Campaign Negativity: RCV may also foster more civil and issue-focused campaigns. Since candidates are vying for voters' second and third preferences, not just their first, they have incentives to avoid overly negative campaigns against opponents and instead focus on policies and issues. This could lead to healthier democratic discourse and more informed voters.

3. Promoting Minority Representation: Independent Redistricting Commissions can potentially improve minority representation by establishing districts that more accurately reflect community demographics. Often, gerrymandering can dilute minority votes by 'packing' them into a single district or 'cracking' them across several districts to limit their influence. Independent redistricting can prevent such tactics and ensure fairer representation.

4. Challenges and Considerations: While both RCV and independent redistricting hold promise, their implementation is not without challenges. For RCV, these include voter education to ensure citizens understand the new voting system, potential initial costs associated with changing voting machinery or systems, and possible legal barriers in some jurisdictions. For independent redistricting, challenges include establishing truly impartial commissions, defining clear and fair criteria for redistricting, and the potential for legal battles over drawn boundaries.

5. Long-term Implications: The potential long-term impacts of these reforms on the political landscape are significant. By increasing the competitiveness of elections, they could lead to greater political diversity, more responsive elected officials, and increased voter engagement and satisfaction. These reforms could fundamentally reshape American democracy for the better, making it more representative and robust.

6. Broadening the Discourse: Lastly, it's crucial to include these types of reforms in the broader discourse on improving the U.S. political system. Ranked-Choice Voting and Independent Redistricting Commissions can

address some key issues, but they are part of a larger conversation that should also include campaign finance reform, lobbying regulation, voter access, and more. By addressing these various elements in tandem, we can work towards a more comprehensive solution to the flaws in the American political system.

Chapter 40

Strengthening Democracy Through Enhanced Voter Access and Lobbying Regulation

Section 1: Enhanced Voter Access

W: One of the cornerstones of a democratic society is the ability of its citizens to participate in the electoral process. Ensuring that every eligible voter has a reasonable and equal opportunity to cast their vote is vital for the legitimacy of any government. Enhanced voter access through simplified voter registration processes, expansion of early voting, and support for mail-in voting can play a critical role in this regard.

Simplified Voter Registration

Automatic voter registration at the Department of Motor Vehicles and other government agencies can significantly increase voter participation. This streamlines the process and helps ensure that changes in address or other information are updated in real-time.

Expansion of Early Voting

Expanding early voting options allows individuals who may not be able to vote on Election Day due to work, caregiving responsibilities, or other commitments to still participate in elections. This is particularly important for those in lower-income brackets who may not have flexible work schedules.

Support for Mail-In Voting

Mail-in voting is critical, especially in the context of natural disasters, public health crises, or for those who are unable to physically go to a polling place. Providing prepaid postage, secure drop boxes, and ensuring timely delivery can make mail-in voting a more accessible option for many.

Section 2: Regulation of Lobbying

While lobbying can be a legitimate and important aspect of the democratic process, when not properly regulated, it can lead to undue influence and corruption. Stricter regulations and greater transparency can mitigate these risks.

Stricter Regulations

Implementing stricter regulations on lobbying could include placing limits on the amount of money that can be spent by lobbying firms, requiring regular disclosure of lobbying activities, and placing restrictions on the 'revolving door' phenomenon where individuals move between government positions and lobbying firms.

Greater Transparency

Transparency in lobbying activities is essential for holding both lobbyists and public officials accountable. This can be achieved through the public disclosure of meetings, contributions, and the specific issues being lobbied for. Transparency allows the public to be informed about who is trying to influence their representatives and on what issues.

In conclusion, by ensuring that the voting process is accessible to all eligible voters and implementing rigorous regulations on lobbying, the integrity and legitimacy of the democratic process can be safeguarded and strengthened. This will contribute to a more representative and responsive government that is accountable to its citizens.

A:

1. Promoting Civic Engagement: Enhanced voter access measures not only increase participation but also promote civic engagement. When individuals have easier and more convenient ways to register and vote, they are more likely to feel a sense of ownership and empowerment in the political process. This can lead to a more

informed and engaged citizenry, fostering a healthier democracy.

2. Addressing Systemic Barriers: Simplified voter registration, expanded early voting, and support for mail-in voting can help address systemic barriers that disproportionately affect marginalized communities. By removing obstacles and providing more options to vote, these measures work towards greater equity and inclusion in the electoral process.

3. Reducing Voter Suppression: Enhancing voter access can help combat voter suppression efforts. By implementing measures that make it easier for individuals to register and vote, voter suppression tactics aimed at discouraging or disenfranchising certain groups can be undermined. This strengthens the democratic principle of equal representation and ensures that every voice is heard.

4. Ethical Lobbying Practices: Stricter regulations and greater transparency in lobbying can contribute to ethical practices and the prevention of undue influence. By holding lobbyists and public officials accountable and shedding light on lobbying activities, the potential for corruption or

improper influence can be minimized. This helps maintain the integrity of the legislative process and safeguards the public interest.

5. Public Trust and Confidence: Implementing enhanced voter access and robust lobbying regulations can help restore public trust and confidence in the political system. When people see that their voices are being heard through accessible voting procedures and that lobbying activities are conducted with transparency and accountability, it strengthens the perception that the system is fair and responsive to the needs and concerns of the citizens.

6. Learning from Best Practices: It is worth studying and learning from the experiences of countries that have successfully implemented measures to enhance voter access and regulate lobbying. Examining international best practices can provide valuable insights and inform the development of effective reforms in the U.S. context.

By prioritizing enhanced voter access and stronger lobbying regulation, the U.S. can foster a more inclusive and accountable democracy. These measures, when combined with other reforms, can contribute to a political system that truly represents the will of the people and upholds the democratic values of equality, transparency, and public participation.

4: Further reflections on these measures might include:

1. Voter Education: In tandem with measures to enhance voter access, a strong emphasis on voter education is essential. Ensuring that citizens understand their rights, how and where to vote, and the issues at stake in an election can maximize the impact of access initiatives. Particularly with changes to voting methods, such as mail-in voting, clear instructions and information are vital.

2. Technological Solutions: Technology could play a role in further enhancing voter access. Online voter registration, digital voting platforms, and mobile apps can make the process more convenient and accessible for many people, especially younger voters. However, such initiatives would need to address concerns around security and voter privacy.

3. Accountability and Oversight: While tightening regulations for lobbying, it's critical to establish robust systems of accountability and oversight. An

independent body, with the power to investigate allegations of misconduct and enforce penalties, could play a key role in ensuring adherence to regulations.

4. Public Financing of Elections: In addition to regulating lobbying, another measure to limit undue influence in politics is the public financing of elections. This can reduce politicians' dependence on large donors and special interests and help level the playing field for candidates with fewer resources.

5. Community Engagement in Rule-making: As regulations are developed to enhance voter access and regulate lobbying, it's crucial to include public and community input. This ensures that policies are grounded in the realities and needs of diverse communities and fosters a sense of public ownership in the democratic process.

6. Resilience to Disinformation: As voter access is expanded, so too can susceptibility to disinformation campaigns. Thus, measures to counteract false information and ensure voters have accurate information about voting

procedures and election issues are increasingly important.

Improving access to voting and regulating lobbying are crucial steps towards a healthier democracy. However, these reforms should be part of a broader strategy to strengthen democratic institutions, foster civic engagement, and ensure a fair and representative political system. This strategy should also be flexible enough to adapt to changing circumstances, such as technological advancements or shifts in voting behaviors, to ensure its continued relevance and effectiveness.

Chapter 41

Public Funding of Campaigns: A Path to Equitable Representation

Introduction

W: One of the fundamental flaws in the United States political system is the enormous influence that money has on politics. This influence often results in a lopsided representation, as candidates with more funding have a better chance of winning elections, regardless of the quality of their policies or representation. A solution that has been proposed to tackle this problem is the exclusive use of public funds to run political campaigns.

Understanding Public Funding of Campaigns

What is Public Funding?

Public funding for campaigns means that candidates receive government funds to finance their campaigns instead of relying on private donations or personal wealth. This approach seeks to level the playing field, reducing the influence of wealthy donors and special interest groups, and allowing candidates to focus more on policy and representation.

Different Models of Public Funding

There are various models of public funding, including:

1. Matching Funds: The government matches small donations made by individuals to candidates.

2. Grants: A lump sum grant is given to candidates who qualify based on certain criteria.

3. Vouchers: Registered voters are given vouchers that they can donate to the candidate(s) of their choice.

Advantages of Public Funding

Reduction in Influence of Big Money

By relying solely on public funds, the influence of large donors and corporations is significantly diminished. This means that politicians are less likely to be beholden to special interests and more likely to act in the public interest.

Encouragement of Diverse Candidates

Public funding can lower the financial barriers to entry for political candidates, encouraging a more diverse range of individuals to run for office. This leads to a more representative democracy.

Focus on Policy and Representation

With financial constraints alleviated, candidates can focus more on developing comprehensive policies and engaging with the electorate, rather than fundraising.

Addressing Flaws in the U.S. Political System

By implementing a public funding model for political campaigns, the United States can address several flaws in its political system:

Influence of Money in Politics: Public funding directly counters the disproportionate influence that wealth can have on political campaigns.

1. Special Interest Influence: Candidates are less likely to be swayed by the interests of large donors and can make decisions based on what is best for their constituents.

2. Economic Barriers to Entry: Reducing the financial burdens associated with campaigning can encourage more candidates from varied backgrounds to participate.

3. Quality of Representation: When candidates can focus on policy over fundraising, the quality of representation and policy development may improve.

Conclusion

Public funding of campaigns represents a paradigm shift in how politics can be conducted in the United States. Through this approach, the political system can move towards a more equitable and representative form of democracy, with a focus on policy and public interest, rather than financial prowess. However, implementing such a system requires careful consideration, legislative support, and public engagement. Additionally, public funding must be complemented by other reforms such as enhanced transparency, electoral reforms, and civic education to realize its full potential in transforming the political landscape.

A:

1. Implementation Challenges: While public funding of campaigns offers potential solutions, there are implementation challenges to consider. Determining the appropriate funding mechanisms, establishing eligibility criteria, and ensuring accountability and transparency in the use of public funds require careful deliberation and effective governance. The system must be designed to prevent misuse and ensure that public funds are allocated equitably and responsibly.

2. Cost and Funding Sources: Public funding of campaigns will require financial resources. Determining the cost and identifying sustainable funding sources, such as dedicated public funds or redirected resources, is essential. Balancing the need for adequate funding with other public priorities requires careful consideration and possibly the involvement of independent oversight bodies to ensure fiscal responsibility.

3. Maintaining Free Speech and Political Competition: Critics of public funding express concerns about potential restrictions on free speech and the possibility of limiting political competition. Striking a balance between promoting equitable representation and protecting constitutional rights is crucial. Adequate safeguards should be in place to ensure that the public funding system does not unduly restrict the ability of candidates and voters to participate in the political process.

4. Public Trust and Confidence: Public funding of campaigns can help restore trust and confidence in the political system by reducing the perception of corruption and undue influence. However, effective communication and transparency about the

process, the allocation of funds, and the impact of public funding on the political landscape are vital. Establishing independent oversight and reporting mechanisms can enhance public trust and ensure accountability.

5. Complementary Reforms: While public funding of campaigns can address the influence of money in politics, it should be part of a comprehensive set of reforms. Strengthening campaign finance regulations, improving transparency and disclosure requirements for political donations, and addressing other systemic issues like gerrymandering and voter suppression are necessary to create a more equitable and inclusive political system.

In conclusion, public funding of campaigns offers a promising avenue to address the flaws associated with the influence of money in politics. By reducing the reliance on private donations and leveling the playing field, it can promote a more representative and responsive democracy. However, careful planning, stakeholder engagement, and complementary reforms are essential to ensure the successful implementation and long-term sustainability of such a system.

4: Additional considerations include:

1. International Examples: Many countries worldwide, such as Germany, Canada, and France, have implemented some form of public funding for political campaigns. Looking at their experiences, successes, and challenges could provide useful insights and lessons for the U.S. as it considers similar reforms.

2. Potential for Biased Allocation: Depending on how public funds are allocated, there could be a risk of entrenching existing power structures. For instance, if funding is based on previous election results, new and emerging parties or independent candidates may be disadvantaged. It's important to ensure a fair system that allows for dynamic political competition.

3. Voter Engagement: Public funding could potentially increase voter engagement by encouraging candidates to focus on policy discussions and community outreach rather than fundraising. But this can also be influenced by other factors such as voter education, accessibility of voting, and overall political culture.

4. Managing Public Perception: While public funding of campaigns can reduce the influence of big money in politics, it may also

be viewed by some as an inappropriate use of taxpayer dollars, especially in times of fiscal restraint or economic hardship. Clear communication on the benefits of public funding, and demonstrated commitment to responsible use of these funds, will be crucial to gain public support.

5. Lobbying and Post-Election Influence: While public funding can help level the playing field during elections, it doesn't necessarily address the influence of money post-election, such as lobbying activities by special interest groups. Comprehensive reform should also include robust lobbying regulations to ensure that political decision-making remains free from undue influence.

Public funding of campaigns could potentially be a game-changer in reducing the influence of big money in politics and promoting more equitable representation. However, a shift of this magnitude would require strong political will, sustained public engagement, and a well-thought-out implementation strategy. With careful design and execution, it could be a significant step towards a more inclusive and responsive democracy in the United States.

Chapter 42

Innovative Workarounds to Address the Flaws in the U.S. Political System

W: In this chapter, we will delve into various innovative workarounds that can address and mitigate some of the fundamental flaws in the U.S. political system. From the influence of money in politics to the limitations imposed by the two-party system, these workarounds aim to empower citizens and restructure political mechanisms to foster a more democratic, inclusive, and effective government. Through methods like harnessing collective intellect, enhancing voter accessibility, and reevaluating electoral processes, this chapter provides insights into how the political landscape can be reformed for the betterment of all citizens.

"Database of Ideas" - A Potential Game Changer

One of the innovative workarounds is the "Database of Ideas" concept. This method emphasizes the power of collective intellect to influence the political process and, in turn, helps in focusing more on the character of individuals running for office.

Here's how it works:

Step #1: Citizens submit ideas on how to improve the government.

Step #2: These ideas are made available for everyone to vote on.

Step #3: The "Database of Ideas" then endorses and supports politicians and political candidates who commit to prioritizing and advocating for the Top-Ten Voted Ideas.

William Search, a proponent of this method, believes that two things make up a good politician:

1. The ideas they have
2. Their moral compass

He argues that by focusing on ideas, the "Database of Ideas" effectively addresses the first point, taking advantage of the collective intellect of the people.

Addressing the Two-Party System and Money in Politics

The two-party system in the United States often offers binary options on complex issues. However, what if both parties have valuable ideas? The "Database of Ideas" presents an opportunity to overcome the limitations of the two-party system by consolidating ideas from a broad spectrum.

Moreover, the "Database of Ideas" can also work as a counter to the influence of money in politics. Since it's centered around ideas, rather than funding, it reduces the emphasis on campaign contributions and focuses on the merit of policies.

Focusing on the Character

With the "Database of Ideas" addressing the issue of ideas in politics, it allows the public to focus more on the character of the individuals running for office. A candidate's character, including their moral compass, becomes a significant factor in evaluating their suitability for office. This results in a political system where policies are shaped by the collective intellect and politicians are valued for their character.

Revisiting the Fundamental Essence of Political Parties

It is important to recognize that a political party, in its purest form, is fundamentally a collection of ideas. These ideas represent various policies, stances, and philosophies aimed at guiding governance and societal development. However, over time, parties can become encumbered by various factors such as special interests, factionalism, and an excessive focus on winning elections, often detracting from the core ideals they are meant to represent.

The "Database of Ideas" workaround serves as a conduit to realign political engagement with this foundational essence of political parties. By focusing primarily on ideas and allowing a broad spectrum of individuals to contribute and vote on these ideas, it embodies the notion of a political party in its purest form.

This approach not only encourages active participation from the citizenry but also ensures that the ideas which gain prominence and support are those that resonate with a wider cross-section of the population.

It paves the way for an evolved form of political engagement, where ideas take center stage, unadulterated by the trappings that have historically plagued traditional political parties.

In essence, the "Database of Ideas" can be seen as a modern embodiment of the ideal that political parties should aspire to - a true collection of ideas that are representative of the people's will and dedicated to societal betterment.

Through this, the political process can move closer to its original purpose and foster a more dynamic, responsive, and representative system of governance.

Implications and Challenges

While the "Database of Ideas" offers an innovative approach to mitigating flaws in the U.S. political system, it's not without challenges. The implementation of such a system would require extensive public engagement and education. Additionally, it is essential to ensure that the database itself remains free from the influence of special interests.

Nonetheless, as a workaround to some of the systemic issues in the U.S. political system, the "Database of Ideas" represents a step towards a more democratic and inclusive form of governance. By leveraging collective intelligence and focusing on the moral character of political candidates, it has the potential to enrich the political landscape and empower citizens in the political process.

A:

1. Public Engagement and Education: Implementing a "Database of Ideas" would require a significant effort to engage and educate the public about its purpose and function. Citizens would need to be actively encouraged to submit their ideas and participate in the voting process. Robust public awareness campaigns, community outreach, and educational initiatives would

be crucial to ensure broad participation and a diverse range of ideas.

2. Diverse Representation: The success of the "Database of Ideas" relies on the participation of a diverse range of citizens, including those from different socioeconomic backgrounds, racial and ethnic groups, and regions. Efforts should be made to ensure that underrepresented communities have equal access and opportunities to contribute their ideas and vote on the platform. This will help prevent the perpetuation of existing power imbalances and amplify the voices of marginalized groups.

3. Safeguarding Against Special Interest Influence: Maintaining the integrity of the "Database of Ideas" is essential to ensure that it remains free from undue influence by special interests. Strict regulations and transparency measures would need to be implemented to prevent the manipulation of the platform by powerful entities seeking to advance their own agendas. Regular audits, independent oversight, and strict disclosure are necessary.

4. Balancing Ideas and Implementation: While the "Database of Ideas" focuses on

generating innovative policy proposals, the successful implementation of these ideas is equally important. It is necessary to strike a balance between encouraging creative thinking and considering the practicality, feasibility, and potential consequences of the proposed ideas. Combining the collective intellect with expertise in policy development and implementation can help ensure the effectiveness of the ideas put forth.

5. Evolving the Political Landscape: The implementation of the "Database of Ideas" would represent a fundamental shift in the political landscape, moving away from a system primarily driven by party affiliation and financial resources. It has the potential to create a more inclusive and responsive political environment where policies are shaped by the collective wisdom of the people. However, such a transformation would require careful navigation of institutional barriers, cultural change, and broad-based political will.

In conclusion, the "Database of Ideas" offers an innovative workaround to the flaws in the U.S. political system by harnessing collective intellect and focusing on the character of political candidates. While challenges exist, such an approach has the potential to empower citizens, broaden policy discussions, and promote a more democratic and inclusive form of governance. Implementing and refining this concept would require ongoing collaboration, adaptability, and a commitment to continuous improvement in the pursuit of a more effective and responsive political system.

4: Expanding on these points, we could consider:

1. Harnessing Technology: The "Database of Ideas" could be technologically driven, utilizing modern digital platforms to enable wide participation and easy access. It could incorporate features such as AI-driven analysis to categorize and filter ideas, blockchain technology for transparency and security, and social media integration for broad dissemination and engagement. However, care must be taken to address potential digital divide issues, ensuring those without robust internet access are not left out.

2. Evaluation Mechanism: While the popularity of an idea is a valuable metric, it shouldn't be the only factor in assessing the worth of a proposal. The "Database of Ideas" could benefit from an evaluation mechanism that considers other factors such as feasibility, cost, potential impact, and

consistency with constitutional and human rights principles.

1. Adaptability: As societal needs change, the "Database of Ideas" should be flexible enough to adapt. Regular reviews and updates should be an integral part of its operation to ensure it remains a relevant and effective platform for public policy development.

2. Mitigating Misinformation: In an era where misinformation can spread rapidly, safeguards should be put in place to ensure the "Database of Ideas" doesn't become a platform for promoting misleading or harmful proposals. This might involve a rigorous vetting process, a fact-checking team, and strong community moderation guidelines.

3. Maintaining Momentum: Keeping the public engaged with the "Database of Ideas" over time may be a challenge. Regular updates, responsive feedback mechanisms, and visible implementation of selected ideas could help maintain interest and engagement.

4. Legal and Regulatory Framework: To operationalize and sustain the "Database of Ideas", a supportive legal and regulatory

framework will be necessary. This may include legislation that mandates consideration of top-voted ideas in legislative processes or policy development.

The "Database of Ideas" presents a fascinating experiment in democratic innovation, suggesting a promising direction for mitigating systemic flaws in the U.S. political system. However, the journey from concept to reality will be filled with challenges, requiring careful planning, strong commitment, and inclusive participation from all stakeholders. The prize could be a political system that is more attuned to the ideas and needs of its citizens, fostering a more vibrant and representative democracy.

Conclusion

Chapter 43

Revisiting the Title 'Is it Moral to be a Billionaire?' and A Call to Action

W: At the outset of this book, I introduced the title 'Is it Moral to be a Billionaire?'. Upon hearing this, my wife remarked that we shouldn't 'Judge' billionaires. This comment made me ponder the distinction between assessing the economic system and judging individuals who have amassed vast wealth.

Evaluating Systems, Not Individuals

It is vital to recognize that this book does not aim to pass judgement on individual billionaires. It's not an indictment of personal achievements or aspirations. Instead, it reflects a critical examination of the economic and political systems that enable massive wealth accumulation at the top while leaving many struggling. In essence, this book is a discourse on the morality of the structures and systems within capitalism, rather than the morality of individuals.

Capitalism With Checks and Balances

Capitalism, as an economic system, has shown to be effective in driving innovation, entrepreneurship, and prosperity. However, like any system, it requires checks and balances to ensure it remains equitable and sustainable for all members of society. Two significant aspects of these checks and balances are a highly progressive tax structure and strengthening unions.

Over the last 50 years, there has been a marked erosion in these checks and balances. Tax structures have often become less progressive, and the strength and influence of labor unions have diminished. The removal of these safeguards has contributed to a skewing of wealth distribution, with a disproportionate concentration of resources amongst the top 1%.

The Role of Money and Resource Allocation

Money, in its essence, is a tool for allocating resources within society. When immense wealth accumulates in the hands of a few, it signifies an allocation of a large portion of society's resources to a small segment. This allocation has ramifications on the quality of life, opportunities, and societal participation for the rest of the population. The current trajectory of resource allocation is neither sustainable nor fair, particularly for future generations.

A Call to Action

This book aims to be more than just an analysis; it seeks to be a call to action. By identifying the flaws in the current systems and suggesting viable solutions, it hopes to incite meaningful dialogue and, more importantly, catalyze change. To create an economy that is not just efficient but also just, it is imperative that we critically assess and reform the systems in place. The focus should be on building a more inclusive, equitable, and sustainable economic structure that serves the interests of all members of society, now and in the future.

Conclusion

As we arrive at the conclusion of "Is It Moral to be a Billionaire?", we are left with profound insights into the complex intersections of wealth, ethics, and societal structure. Together, we have embarked on an enlightening exploration, guided by the experiences of author William Search, and the collaborative intelligence of AI interlocutors, chatGPT 3.5 and chatGPT 4.0.

We've dissected the stark economic disparities represented by Search's personal encounters with an employer who favored wealth accumulation over employee welfare. We've contrasted the relative financial stability of union-backed workers from the past to the challenges faced by today's educated workforce, underscoring the changing landscape of labor and wealth distribution.

Throughout our exploration, we've dissected the components of billionaire creation — skill, fortune, or systemic exploitation. We've uncovered how concentrated wealth can alter political landscapes, weaken labor unions, and foster regressive tax policies that further wealth inequality. Moreover, we've scrutinized potential remedies such as the Universal Basic Income, tax reform, and the revitalization of labor unions.

Our journey also led us to the dark side of wealth accumulation: the exploitative utilization of racial and cultural divisions to fragment the working class, the psychological toll of excessive wealth, and the socio-economic disruptions caused by unrestricted wealth accumulation.

In addressing these issues, we've proposed innovative solutions. We discussed the benefits of decoupling politics from finance, implementing progressive taxation, and charting a proactive path towards a more balanced distribution of resources.

Drawing from Search's earlier works, we expanded the dialogue on morality as humanity's purpose, integrating it into our broader discourse on wealth and inequality.

In conclusion, "Is It Moral to be a Billionaire?" has sought to provoke thought, invite discourse, and challenge preconceived notions. We hope that, as a reader, you leave this exploration with a refreshed understanding of wealth, morality, and society. More importantly, we hope it has empowered you to engage in continued conversations about these vital issues and take part in the collective effort to foster a more equitable world.

Sources

- National Bureau of Economic Research. (2016). Household Wealth Trends in the United States, 1962-2016: Has Middle Class Wealth Recovered? Retrieved from https://www.nber.org/papers/w24085

- CBS This Morning. (2023). A Visualization of America's Wealth Inequality. CBS News. Retrieved from https://www.cbsnews.com/news/wealth-inequality-visualization/

- Piketty, T. (2014). Capital in the Twenty-First Century. Harvard University Press.

- Page, B., Seawright, J., & Lacombe, M. (2018). Billionaires and Stealth Politics. University of Chicago Press.

- Harrington, B. (2016). Capital Without Borders: Wealth Managers and the One Percent. Harvard University Press.

- Gilens, M., & Page, B.I. (2014). Testing Theories of American Politics: Elites, Interest Groups, and Average Citizens. Perspectives on Politics, 12(3), 564-581. DOI: 10.1017/S1537592714001595

- Scheiber, N. (2018). Billionaires vs. the Press in the Era of Trump. The New York Times. Retrieved from

- https://www.nytimes.com/2018/11/25/business/media/billionaires-vs-press.html
- Page, B., Seawright, J., & Lacombe, M. (2018). Billionaires and Stealth Politics. University of Chicago Press.
- Harrington, B. (2016). Capital Without Borders: Wealth Managers and the One Percent. Harvard University Press.
- Gilens, M., & Page, B.I. (2014). Testing Theories of American Politics: Elites, Interest Groups, and Average Citizens. Perspectives on Politics, 12(3), 564-581. DOI: 10.1017/S1537592714001595
- Zakaria, F. (2015). The rise of the new global elite. The Atlantic. Retrieved from https://www.theatlantic.com/magazine/archive/2011/01/the-rise-of-the-new-global-elite/308343/
- Anand, A., & Segal, P. (2015). The global distribution of income. Handbook of Income Distribution, 2, 937-979. DOI: 10.1016/B978-0-444-59428-0.00015-3
- Silva, Derek. "Who benefited most from the Tax Cuts and Jobs Act?" Policygenius, December 28, 2021, https://www.policygenius.com/taxes/who-benefited-most-from-the-tax-cuts-and-jobs-act/
- Page, Benjamin I., Seawright, Jason, and Lacombe, Matthew J. "Billionaires and Stealth Politics." University of Chicago Press, 2018.

- Harrington, Brooke. "Capital without Borders: Wealth Managers and the One Percent." Harvard University Press, 2016.

- Gilens, Martin, and Page, Benjamin I. "Testing Theories of American Politics: Elites, Interest Groups, and Average Citizens." Perspectives on Politics, vol. 12, no. 3, 2014, pp. 564–581.

- Scheiber, Noam. "Limiting the Influence of Tech When You Report on It." The New York Times, November 27, 2018, https://www.nytimes.com/2018/11/27/business/labor-technology-news-media.html

- United States, Congress, "Tax Cuts and Jobs Act." Congress.gov, https://www.congress.gov/bill/115th-congress/house-bill/1

- United States, Department of the Treasury, Internal Revenue Service. "SOI Tax Stats - Historic Table 2." IRS, https://www.irs.gov/statistics/soi-tax-stats-historic-table-2

- United States, Government Accountability Office. "2018 Tax Filing: Most Taxpayers Found New Tax Law Beneficial." GAO, https://www.gao.gov/assets/710/704408.pdf

- The Bible, New International Version. Matthew 6:24. BibleGateway. https://www.biblegateway.com/passage/?search=Matthew+6%3A24&version=NIV

- The Quran, Surah Al-Hakumut-Takathur (102:1-2). Quran.com. https://quran.com/102
- The Tanakh, Jewish Publication Society. Proverbs 28:25. Sefaria. https://www.sefaria.org/Proverbs.28.25?lang=bi&with=all&lang2=en
- The Bhagavad Gita, 16.21. Bhagavad-Gita Trust. http://www.bhagavad-gita.org/Gita/verse-16-20.html
- The Buddhist Texts. The Four Noble Truths. Access to Insight (BCBS Edition). https://www.accesstoinsight.org/ptf/dhamma/sacca/index.html
- Guru Granth Sahib. Sri Granth. http://www.srigranth.org/servlet/gurbani.gurbani?Action=KeertanPage
- Tao Te Ching, Stephen Mitchell Translation. https://taoteching.org.uk/index.php?c=1&a=Stephen+Mitchell
- The Analects of Confucius. The Internet Classics Archive by Daniel C. Stevenson, Web Atomics. http://classics.mit.edu/Confucius/analects.html
- The Avesta. The Internet Sacred Text Archive. http://www.sacred-texts.com/zor/
- The Teachings of Jainism. Jainworld. https://www.jainworld.com/jainbooks/teachings.htm

- The Baha'i Faith. Writings of Baha'u'llah. Bahai.org. https://www.bahai.org/library/authoritative-texts/bahaullah/

- The Teachings of Shinto. BBC Religions. http://www.bbc.co.uk/religion/religions/shinto/beliefs/beliefs.shtml

- Plato, The Republic. London: Penguin Classics, 2007.

- Aristotle, Nicomachean Ethics. New York: Oxford University Press, 2009.

- Epicurus, Letters and Sayings of Epicurus. New York: Barnes & Noble, 2005.

- Seneca, Letters from a Stoic. London: Penguin Classics, 2004.

- Epictetus, Discourses and Selected Writings. London: Penguin Classics, 2008.

- Marcus Aurelius, Meditations. New York: Modern Library, 2002.

- Garfield, Jay L. The Fundamental Wisdom of the Middle Way: Nagarjuna's Mulamadhyamakakarika. New York: Oxford University Press, 1995.

- Vasubandhu, Karmasiddhiprakarana: The Treatise on Action by Vasubandhu. Delhi: Motilal Banarsidass Publishers, 1998.

- Marx, Karl, and Friedrich Engels. The Communist Manifesto. London: Penguin Classics, 2002.

- Rawls, John. A Theory of Justice. Massachusetts: Belknap Press, 2005.

- Bonacich, Edna. "Advanced Capitalism and Black/White Race Relations in the United States: A Split Labor Market Interpretation." American Sociological Review, vol. 41, no. 1, 1976, pp. 34-51.

- Du Bois, W. E. B. "Black Reconstruction in America: An Essay Toward a History of the Part Which Black Folk Played in the Attempt to Reconstruct Democracy in America, 1860–1880." Oxford University Press, 1935.

- Haney-López, Ian. "Dog Whistle Politics: How Coded Racial Appeals Have Reinvented Racism and Wrecked the Middle Class." Oxford University Press, 2014.

- Massey, Douglas S., and Nancy A. Denton. "American Apartheid: Segregation and the Making of the Underclass." Harvard University Press, 1993.

- Oliver, Melvin L., and Thomas M. Shapiro. "Black Wealth/White Wealth: A New Perspective on Racial Inequality." Routledge, 1995.

- Chomsky, Noam. "Media Control: The Spectacular Achievements of Propaganda." Seven Stories Press, 2002.

- Roediger, David R. "Working Toward Whiteness: How America's Immigrants Became White: The Strange Journey from Ellis Island to the Suburbs." Basic Books, 2005.

- Gilens, Martin. "Why Americans Hate Welfare: Race, Media, and the Politics of Antipoverty Policy." University of Chicago Press, 1999.

- Wilson, William J. "When Work Disappears: The World of the New Urban Poor." Knopf, 1996.

- Saez, Emmanuel, and Gabriel Zucman. "The Triumph of Injustice: How the Rich Dodge Taxes and How to Make Them Pay." W. W. Norton & Company, 2019.

- Fisher, Tyler. "How past income tax rate cuts on the wealthy affected the economy." Politico, 27 Sep 2017. [Online] Available at: https://www.politico.com/interactives/2017/gop-tax-rate-cuts-wealthy-economic-growth/

- Piketty, Thomas. "Top Marginal Tax Rates Since 1900." Paris School of Economics. [Online] Available at: https://piketty.pse.ens.fr/files/Piketty2014TOP.pdf

- U.S. Department of the Treasury. "The Revenue Act of 1964." [Online] Available at:

- https://www.treasury.gov/resource-center/faqs/Taxes/Pages/historyr2.aspx
- Congressional Research Service. "Taxes and the Economy: An Economic Analysis of the Top Tax Rates Since 1945." [Online] Available at: https://fas.org/sgp/crs/misc/R42729.pdf
- World Bank. "GDP per capita growth rate." [Online] Available at: https://data.worldbank.org/indicator/NY.GDP.PCAP.KD.ZG
- Trump, Donald J. "Unified Framework For Fixing Our Broken Tax Code." [Online] Available at: https://www.treasury.gov/press-center/press-releases/Documents/Tax-Framework.pdf
- Tax Foundation. "Analysis of Donald Trump's Tax Plan." [Online] Available at: https://taxfoundation.org/article/details-and-analysis-donald-trump-s-tax-plan
- Congressional Research Service. "Temporary Tax Policy and the Budget Process." [Online] Available at: https://fas.org/sgp/crs/misc/R44732.pdf
- Data on top marginal income tax rates: Tax Foundation, "Federal Individual Income Tax Rates History, Nominal Dollars, 1913-2018" (taxfoundation.org)
- Analysis of income tax bias: Saez, Emmanuel, and Gabriel Zucman. "The Triumph of Injustice:

How the Rich Dodge Taxes and How to Make Them Pay." W.W. Norton & Company, 2019.

- Information on regressive state and local taxes: Institute on Taxation and Economic Policy, "Who Pays? A Distributional Analysis of the Tax Systems in All 50 States" (itep.org)

- Discussion on progressivity and the middle class: Piketty, Thomas. "Capital in the Twenty-First Century." Belknap Press, 2014.

- Bureau of Labor Statistics. "Union Members Summary." U.S. Department of Labor, January 21, 2022. Accessed June 15, 2023. https://www.bls.gov/news.release/union2.nr0.htm.

- Bureau of Labor Statistics. "Union Members in 2021 - Technical Note." U.S. Department of Labor, January 21, 2022. Accessed June 15, 2023. https://www.bls.gov/news.release/pdf/union2.pdf.

- Bureau of Labor Statistics. "Union Membership and Coverage Database." U.S. Department of Labor. Accessed June 15, 2023. https://www.bls.gov/ncs/ebs/home.htm.

- Hoxby, Caroline M., and George B. Bulman. "The effects of school desegregation on mixed-race births." Journal of Policy Analysis and Management 36, no. 2 (2017): 269-293.

- Western, Bruce, and Jake Rosenfeld. "Unions, Norms, and the Rise in U.S. Wage Inequality."

American Sociological Review 76, no. 4 (2011): 513-537.

- Milkman, Ruth, Stephanie Luce, and Penny Lewis. "Changing the Subject: A Bottom-Up Account of Occupy Wall Street in New York City." Perspectives on Work 17, no. 1 (2013): 23-26.

- Fletcher, Bill, and Martha Burk. "Do Public Employee Pensions Serve the Common Good? The Case of Teacher Pensions." Journal of Labor Research 40, no. 3 (2019): 263-289.

- "AFL-CIO." AFL-CIO. Accessed June 15, 2023. https://aflcio.org/.

- "Change to Win Federation." Change to Win Federation. Accessed June 15, 2023. https://changetowin.org/.

- Gould, Elise, and Will Kimball. "Unions help narrow the gender wage gap." Economic Policy Institute, Briefing Paper #483 (2019).

- Farber, Henry S., Daniel Herbst, Ilyana Kuziemko, and Suresh Naidu. "Unions and Inequality Over the Twentieth Century: New Evidence from Survey Data." The Quarterly Journal of Economics 133, no. 1 (2018): 379-425.

- Mishel, Lawrence, and Kar-Fai Gee. "State of Working America Wages 2019: A Story of Slow, Unequal, and Unsteady Wage Growth over the Last 40 Years." Economic Policy Institute (2019).

- Freeman, Richard B. "What Do Unions Do? A 20-Year Perspective." ILR Review 46, no. 3 (1993): 352-365.

- Card, David, and Alan B. Krueger. "Minimum Wages and Employment: A Case Study of the Fast-Food Industry in New Jersey and Pennsylvania." American Economic Review 84, no. 4 (1994): 772-793.

- Freeman, Richard B., and James L. Medoff. "What Do Unions Do?: Basic Books," 1984.

- Western, Bruce, and Jake Rosenfeld. "Unions, Norms, and the Rise in U.S. Wage Inequality." American Sociological Review 76, no. 4 (2011): 513-537.

- Farber, H. S., Herbst, D., Kuziemko, I., & Naidu, S. (2018). Unions and inequality over the twentieth century: New evidence from survey data. NBER Working Paper No. 24587. National Bureau of Economic Research.

- Flavin, P., & Hartney, M. T. (2019). From Inequality to Action: The Role of Worker Voice in the Labor Policy Process. RSF: The Russell Sage Foundation Journal of the Social Sciences, 5(5), 127-150.

- Weil, D. (2014). The Fissured Workplace: Why Work Became So Bad for So Many and What Can Be Done to Improve It. Harvard University Press.

- Ghilarducci, T., Farmand, A., & Papadopoulos, M. (2020). Bargaining Power Index – 2020 Update: Workers and Unions Lose Power as Monopsony Power Rises. Schwartz Center for Economic Policy Analysis and Department of Economics, The New School for Social Research.

- Goldfield, M. (1987). The Decline of Organized Labor in the United States. University Of Chicago Press.

- Collins, B. (2019). The Legislative Attack on American Wages and Labor Standards, 2011–2012. Economic Policy Institute.

- Greenhouse, S. (2019). Beaten Down, Worked Up: The Past, Present, and Future of American Labor. Knopf.

- Autor, D., Dorn, D., & Hanson, G. (2013). The China Syndrome: Local Labor Market Effects of Import Competition in the United States. American Economic Review, 103(6), 2121-2168.

- Bureau of Labor Statistics (BLS). (various years). Union Members Summary. U.S. Department of Labor.

- Taft-Hartley Act of 1947. Public Law 80-101.

- National Labor Relations Board (NLRB). (various years). Annual Reports. U.S. Government Printing Office.

- United States Supreme Court. (various years). U.S. Reports. U.S. Government Printing Office.

- Logan, J. (2006). The Union Avoidance Industry in the United States. British Journal of Industrial Relations, 44(4), 651-675.

- Arntz, M., Gregory, T., & Zierahn, U. (2016). The Risk of Automation for Jobs in OECD Countries: A Comparative Analysis. OECD Social, Employment and Migration Working Papers, No. 189, OECD Publishing, Paris.

- "The Equality of the Senate and the Inequality of the States" - Harvard Law Review, July 2022: https://www.harvardlawreview.org/2022/07/equality-senate-inequality-states/

- "The Senate's Rural Skew Makes It Very Hard For Democrats To Win The Supreme Court" - FiveThirtyEight, September 2020: https://fivethirtyeight.com/features/the-senates-rural-skew-makes-it-very-hard-for-democrats-to-win-the-supreme-court/

- "Filibuster and Cloture" - U.S. Senate: https://www.senate.gov/about/powers-procedures/filibusters-cloture.htm

- "The Impact of the Senate's 60-Vote Threshold" - Brookings, May 2021: https://www.brookings.edu/blog/fixgov/2021/05/27/impact-senate-60-vote-threshold/

- "The Math Behind the Senate and Filibusters" - The New York Times, March 2023: https://www.nytimes.com/2023/03/15/us/politics/senate-filibuster-math.html

- Brynjolfsson, E., & McAfee, A. (2014). The Second Machine Age: Work, Progress, and Prosperity in a Time of Brilliant Technologies. W.W. Norton & Company.

- Chui, M., Manyika, J., & Miremadi, M. (2016). Where machines could replace humans—and where they can't (yet). McKinsey Quarterly.

- Furman, J., & Seamans, R. (2019). AI and the Economy. Innovation Policy and the Economy, 19(1), 161–191.

- Korinek, A., & Stiglitz, J. (2017). Artificial intelligence and its implications for income distribution and unemployment. NBER Working Paper No. 24174

- Dobbs, Lou. (2004). Exporting America: Why Corporate Greed Is Shipping American Jobs Overseas. Warner Business Books.

- Mankiw, N. G. (2004). Principles of Economics (3rd ed.). Thomson South-Western.

- Krugman, P. (2009). The Return of Depression Economics and the Crisis of 2008. W.W. Norton & Company.

- Taylor, Timothy. (2011). The Instant Economist: Everything You Need to Know About How the Economy Works. Plume.

- Economic Policy Institute. (Various years). Various publications and research on outsourcing and offshoring.

- Bardhan, Ashok Deo, & Kroll, Cynthia. (2003). The New Wave of Outsourcing. Fisher Center Research Reports: 1103.

- McKinsey Global Institute. (2017). Jobs Lost, Jobs Gained: Workforce Transitions in a Time of Automation.

- World Economic Forum. (2018). The Future of Jobs Report 2018.

- Susskind, D. (2020). A World Without Work: Technology, Automation and How We Should Respond. Metropolitan Books.

- Elsig, Claudia M., MD. (2022). The Psychology of Wealth and How It Affects Mental Health.

- Ali, A., & Kubba, H. (2022, July 1). Are billionaires just lucky? Billionaires have an unfair advantage–so do you. Fortune. Retrieved from https://fortune.com/2022/07/01/billionaires-just-lucky-success-entrepreneurs-careers-elon-musk-startups-ali-kubba/amp/

- Duverger, M. (1954). "Political Parties: Their Organization and Activity in the Modern State." Wiley.

- Fiorina, M. P., & Abrams, S. J. (2008). "Political Polarization in the American Public." Annual Review of Political Science, 11, 563–588.

- Abramowitz, A., & Saunders, K. (2008). "Is Polarization a Myth?" Journal of Politics, 70(2), 542–555.

- Reilly, B. (2002). "Social Choice in the South Seas: Electoral Innovation and the Borda Count in the Pacific Island Countries." International Political Science Review, 23(4), 355-372.
- Kirschenbaum, Julia, and Michael Li. "Gerrymandering Explained." Brennan Center for Justice, Last updated June 9, 2023. https://www.brennancenter.org/our-work/research-reports/gerrymandering-explained
- "Rucho v. Common Cause." Oyez, https://www.oyez.org/cases/2018/18-422
- "The Freedom to Vote Act." Brennan Center for Justice, https://www.brennancenter.org/our-work/policy-solutions/freedom-vote-act
- "The Electoral College: A 2020 Presidential Election Timeline", Congressional Research Service, Updated December 3, 2020: https://crsreports.congress.gov/product/pdf/IF/IF11641
- "The Electoral College", National Conference of State Legislatures, February 3, 2021: https://www.ncsl.org/research/elections-and-campaigns/the-electoral-college.aspx
- "How the Electoral College Became Winner-Take-All", FairVote, https://www.fairvote.org/how-the-electoral-college-became-winner-take-all

- "Electoral College Reform: Contemporary Issues for Congress", Congressional Research Service, Updated March 8, 2021: https://crsreports.congress.gov/product/pdf/R/R46465

- "Origins and Development of the Electoral College", National Archives and Records Administration, https://www.archives.gov/electoral-college/about

- "Understanding the Presidential Election Process", Department of Homeland Security, November 18, 2020: https://www.dhs.gov/how-do-i/understand-presidential-election-process

- Lessig, L. (2011). "Republic, Lost: How Money Corrupts Congress—and a Plan to Stop It". Twelve. ISBN: 9780446576437.

- "Supreme Court Case: Citizens United v. Federal Election Commission". History, Art & Archives, U.S. House of Representatives. Retrieved from https://history.house.gov/Historical-Highlights/2000-/The-Supreme-Court-case-Citizens-United-v--Federal-Election-Commission/

- Confessore, N., Cohen, S., Yourish, K. (2016). "Buying Power: The Families Funding the 2016 Presidential Election". The New York Times. Retrieved from https://www.nytimes.com/interactive/2015/1

0/11/us/politics/2016-presidential-election-super-pac-donors.html

- Mayer, J. (2016). "Dark Money: The Hidden History of the Billionaires Behind the Rise of the Radical Right". Doubleday. ISBN: 9780385535595.

- "The Color of Money: How White Contributors Amplify Inequality". Demos, 2021. Retrieved from https://www.demos.org/research/color-money-how-white-contributors-amplify-inequality

- "Campaign Finance: Laws & Regulations". Brennan Center for Justice, 2020. Retrieved from https://www.brennancenter.org/our-work/research-reports/campaign-finance-laws-regulations

- Corrado, A. (2005). "Money and Politics: A History of Federal Campaign Finance Law". In: The New Campaign Finance Sourcebook. Brookings Institution Press. ISBN: 0815751252.

- "Term Limits and the Need for a Citizen Legislature." US Term Limits, 2023. https://www.termlimits.com/why-term-limits/

- Edwards, George C. "Why Term Limits Should Be Opposed." National Affairs, 2013. https://www.nationalaffairs.com/publications/detail/why-term-limits-should-be-opposed

- Jones, Jeffrey M. "U.S. Term Limits: Widespread Support, Little Action." Gallup, 2021. https://news.gallup.com/poll/16568/us-term-limits-widespread-support-little-action.aspx

- Gersen, Jeannie Suk. "Term Limits and the Cult of the Presidency." The New Yorker, 2022. https://www.newyorker.com/news/our-columnists/term-limits-and-the-cult-of-the-presidency

- Fisher, Louis. "The Case Against the Repeal of the 22nd Amendment Concerning Presidential Term Limits." CATO Institute, 1997. https://www.cato.org/publications/congressional-testimony/case-against-repeal-22nd-amendment-concerning-presidential-term-limits

- Pierson, Paul. "Dismantling the Welfare State? Reagan, Thatcher, and the Politics of Retrenchment." Cambridge University Press, 1994.

- "Short-term thinking in business: causes, effects, and potential solutions." Mckinsey & Company, 2017. https://www.mckinsey.com/business-functions/strategy-and-corporate-finance/our-insights/the-case-against-corporate-short-termism

- Barber, M., & McCarty, N. (2015). Causes and Consequences of Polarization. In J. Mansbridge & C. J. Martin (Eds.), Political Negotiation: A Handbook. Brookings Institution Press.

- Fiorina, M. P., & Abrams, S. J. (2008). Political Polarization in the American Public. Annual Review of Political Science, 11, 563-588.

- McCarty, N., Poole, K. T., & Rosenthal, H. (2006). Polarized America: The Dance of Ideology and Unequal Riches. MIT Press.

- West, D. M. (2017). Political polarization, presidential leadership, and cross-party collaboration. In Leadership and Global Governance (pp. 151-167). Routledge.

- Hetherington, M. J. (2009). Putting Polarization in Perspective. Daedalus, 138(2), 67-81.

- "Citizens United v. Federal Election Commission." Oyez. Accessed June 20, 2023. https://www.oyez.org/cases/2008/08-205

- "The Distortion of American Politics by Big Money." Harvard Law Review. Accessed June 20, 2023. https://harvardlawreview.org/2015/03/the-distortion-of-american-politics-by-big-money/

- "The Role of Lobbyists in American Politics." The Journal of Politics. Accessed June 20, 2023. https://www.journals.uchicago.edu/doi/full/10.1086/677441

- "Revolving Door: How Security Clearances Perpetuate Top-Level Corruption in the United States." Yale Law Journal. Accessed June 20, 2023.

- https://www.yalelawjournal.org/forum/revolving-door
- "Money in Politics: Campaign Finance Reform." Brennan Center for Justice. Accessed June 20, 2023. https://www.brennancenter.org/issues/reform-money-politics
- "Lobbying: Persuasion, or just Paying for Policy?" National Bureau of Economic Research. Accessed June 20, 2023. https://www.nber.org/digest/jun10/lobbying-persuasion-or-just-paying-policy
- "Voter Identification Requirements | Voter ID Laws." National Conference of State Legislatures. Accessed on June 16, 2023. https://www.ncsl.org/research/elections-and-campaigns/voter-id.aspx
- "The Impact of Strict Voter ID Laws on Minority Turnout." Brennan Center for Justice. Accessed on June 16, 2023. https://www.brennancenter.org/our-work/research-reports/impact-strict-voter-id-laws-minority-turnout
- "Polling Place Closure and Vote Suppression." Civil Rights.org. Accessed on June 16, 2023. https://civilrights.org/democracy-diverted-polling-place-closures-and-the-right-to-vote/
- "The State of Voting Rights Litigation (Summer 2023)." Brennan Center for Justice. Accessed on June 16, 2023.

- https://www.brennancenter.org/our-work/research-reports/state-voting-rights-litigation-summer-2023
- "Voting Rights for Elderly and Disabled People." American Civil Liberties Union. Accessed on June 16, 2023. https://www.aclu.org/issues/voting-rights/voter-restoration/voting-rights-elderly-and-disabled-people
- "Ranked-Choice Voting and its Impact on Democracy." FairVote. https://www.fairvote.org/research_rcv
- "Why We Need Ranked Choice Voting." RepresentUs. https://represent.us/why-we-need-ranked-choice-voting/
- "The Case for Independent Redistricting Commissions." Brennan Center for Justice. https://www.brennancenter.org/our-work/research-reports/case-independent-redistricting-commissions
- "How Do Independent Redistricting Commissions Work?" National Conference of State Legislatures. https://www.ncsl.org/research/redistricting/what-do-we-mean-by-independent-redistricting-commission.aspx
- Brennan Center for Justice. (2020). Automatic Voter Registration. Retrieved from https://www.brennancenter.org/our-

work/research-reports/automatic-voter-registration

- National Conference of State Legislatures. (2021). Early Voting. Retrieved from https://www.ncsl.org/research/elections-and-campaigns/early-voting-in-state-elections.aspx
- U.S. Election Assistance Commission. (2017). Vote by Mail. Retrieved from https://www.eac.gov/voters/vote-by-mail
- La Raja, Raymond J. (2014). Lobbying and Transparency: The Complexity of Compliance in a Global Economy. Interest Groups & Advocacy, 3, 238–261. doi:10.1057/iga.2014.15
- Center for Responsive Politics. (2021). Revolving Door. Retrieved from https://www.opensecrets.org/revolving/
- Campaign Legal Center. (2019). Strengthening Democracy Through Lobbying Reform. Retrieved from https://campaignlegal.org/update/strengthening-democracy-through-lobbying-reform
- Malbin, Michael J. "Public Funding of Elections: What Does Public Financing Do, and How Do We Know?." The Forum. Vol. 13. No. 4. De Gruyter, 2016. https://www.degruyter.com/document/doi/10.1515/for-2016-0012/html
- Overton, Spencer. "Matching Political Contributions." George Washington Law

Review, vol. 96, no. 5, 2013. https://scholarship.law.gwu.edu/cgi/viewcontent.cgi?article=2430&context=faculty_publications

- Garrett, R. Sam. "Public Financing of Presidential Campaigns: Overview and Analysis." Congressional Research Service, 2019. https://fas.org/sgp/crs/misc/R43976.pdf
- Hasen, Richard L. "Clipping Coupons for Democracy: An Egalitarian/Public Choice Defense of Campaign Finance Vouchers." Journal of Law and Politics, vol. 84, 1996. https://scholarship.law.uci.edu/cgi/viewcontent.cgi?article=1228&context=faculty_scholarship
- Torres-Spelliscy, Ciara. "The $500 Revolution: A Small Donor Public Financing Revolution." Brennan Center for Justice, 2016. https://www.brennancenter.org/our-work/research-reports/500-revolution
- "Empowering Small Donors in Federal Elections." Brennan Center for Justice, 2012. https://www.brennancenter.org/our-work/research-reports/empowering-small-donors-federal-elections
- Zucman, Gabriel, and Saez, Emmanuel. "The Hidden Wealth of Nations: The Scourge of Tax Havens." University of Chicago Press, 2015. https://press.uchicago.edu/ucp/books/book/chicago/H/bo20652614.html

- "Policy Basics: Where Do Federal Tax Revenues Come From?" Center on Budget and Policy Priorities, 9 Apr. 2019, https://www.cbpp.org/research/federal-tax/policy-basics-where-do-federal-tax-revenues-come-from.

- Saez, Emmanuel, and Zucman, Gabriel. "Progressive Wealth Taxation." Brookings Papers on Economic Activity, Fall 2019. https://www.brookings.edu/wp-content/uploads/2019/09/Saez-Zucman_conference-draft.pdf

- Gale, William G., and Slemrod, Joel. "Rethinking Estate and Gift Taxation." Brookings Institution Press, 2001. https://www.brookings.edu/book/rethinking-estate-and-gift-taxation/

- Burman, Leonard E. "The Capital Gains Tax Preference." Tax Policy Center, 24 Feb. 2020. https://www.taxpolicycenter.org/taxvox/capital-gains-tax-preference

- "The Distribution of Wealth in America, 1983-2013." Congressional Budget Office, Dec. 2018, https://www.cbo.gov/publication/54646.

- Saez, Emmanuel, and Gabriel Zucman. "The Triumph of Injustice: How the Rich Dodge Taxes and How to Make Them Pay." W.W. Norton & Company, 2019. https://www.wwnorton.com/books/9781324002727

- Piketty, Thomas. "Capital in the Twenty-First Century." Harvard University Press, 2014. http://www.hup.harvard.edu/catalog.php?isbn=9780674430006
- Internal Revenue Service. "Progressive Tax System." IRS, https://www.irs.gov/government-entities/federal-state-local-governments/federal-taxation-of-municipal-bond-interest-for-individuals
- Urban-Brookings Tax Policy Center. "Wealth Transfer Taxes." https://www.taxpolicycenter.org/briefing-book/what-are-wealth-transfer-taxes-and-how-do-they-work
- Congressional Research Service. "An Introduction to the U.S. Income Tax System and Tax Reform Debate." CRS, 2019. https://crsreports.congress.gov/product/pdf/R/R45729
- Summers, Lawrence, and Natasha Sarin. "A 'wealth tax' presents a revenue estimation puzzle." The Washington Post, 2019. https://www.washingtonpost.com/opinions/2019/04/04/wealth-tax-presents-revenue-estimation-puzzle
- Avi-Yonah, Reuven S., and Kimberly A. Clausing. "Reforming corporate taxation in a global economy: A proposal to adopt formulary apportionment." In Path to Prosperity, pp. 319-

344. 2007. https://www.brookings.edu/wp-content/uploads/2016/06/06corporatetaxes_clausing.pdf

- Gravelle, Jane G. "Tax Havens: International Tax Avoidance and Evasion." Congressional Research Service, 2015. https://fas.org/sgp/crs/misc/R40623.pdf
- Slemrod, Joel. "Taxing Ourselves: A Citizen's Guide to the Debate over Taxes." MIT Press, 2008. https://mitpress.mit.edu/books/taxing-ourselves
- Auerbach, Alan J. "A modern corporate tax." Center for American Progress, 2010.

  https://www.americanprogress.org/issues/economy/reports/2010/12/13/8763/a-modern-corporate-tax/
- Kleinbard, Edward D. "Through a Latte, Darkly: Starbucks's Stateless Income Planning." Tax Notes 139 (2013): 1515. https://papers.ssrn.com/sol3/papers.cfm?abstract_id=2264388
- Murphy, Richard. "The Tax Gap: Tax Evasion in 2014 and What Can Be Done About It." Public and Commercial Services Union, 2014. https://www.taxresearch.org.uk/Documents/PCSTaxGap2014Full.pdf
- "Basic Income: A Radical Proposal for a Free Society and a Sane Economy" by Philippe Van Parijs and Yannick Vanderborght. Published by

Harvard University Press, 2017. https://www.hup.harvard.edu/catalog.php?isbn=9780674052284

- "The War on Normal People: The Truth About America's Disappearing Jobs and Why Universal Basic Income Is Our Future" by Andrew Yang. Published by Hachette Books, 2018. https://www.hachettebookgroup.com/titles/andrew-yang/the-war-on-normal-people/9780316414258/

- "Give People Money: How a Universal Basic Income Would End Poverty, Revolutionize Work, and Remake the World" by Annie Lowrey. Published by Crown, 2018. https://www.penguinrandomhouse.com/books/546260/give-people-money-by-annie-lowrey/

- "Exploring Universal Basic Income: A Guide to Navigating Concepts, Evidence, and Practices" by World Bank Group, 2020. https://openknowledge.worldbank.org/handle/10986/32555

- "The Basic Income Guarantee: Insuring Progress and Prosperity in the 21st Century" by Charles M. A. Clark. Published by Liffey Press, 2002. https://www.bookdepository.com/Basic-Income-Guarantee-Charles-M-Clark/9781904148122

Made in the USA
Las Vegas, NV
30 September 2023